D0388598

...ERTY OF
...IC LIBRARY

A CURIOUS TRAVELER'S GUIDE

Paris

A CURIOUS TRAVELER'S GUIDE

Paris

ELEANOR ALDRIDGE

The Countryman Press
A division of W. W. Norton & Company
Independent Publishers Since 1923

Copyright © 2019 by Eleanor Aldridge

All rights reserved
Printed in the United States of America

All photographs by the author.

For information about permission to reproduce selections
from this book, write to Permissions, The Countryman Press,
500 Fifth Avenue, New York, NY 10110

For information about special discounts for bulk purchases,
please contact W. W. Norton Special Sales at
specialsales@wwnorton.com or 800-233-4830

Manufacturing by Versa Press
Book design by Lidija Tomas
Maps by Mapping Specialists, Ltd.
Production manager: Devon Zahn

The Countryman Press
www.countrymanpress.com

A division of W. W. Norton & Company, Inc.
500 Fifth Avenue, New York, NY 10110
www.wwnorton.com

978-1-68268-388-0 (pbk.)

10 9 8 7 6 5 4 3 2 1

CONTENTS

PARIS

Seine

Boulevard Bineau

Boulevard Périphérique

Boulevard Berthier

Avenue de Clichy

Boule

Avenue Charles de Gaulle

Avenue de Wagram

Boulevard H

Allée de Longchamp

Avenue des Champs-Élysées

Rue de K

1

Boulevard Périphérique

Boulevard Suchet

Avenue de Versailles

2

Boulevard Saint-Ger

Seine

8

Avenue du Maine

9

Boulevard Périphérique

Boulevard Brune

ABOUT THIS GUIDE

Too many visitors focus on a staid tick-list approach to Paris's big attractions, leaving with a wallet of ticket stubs and phone jammed with photos, but little in the way of experiences or glimpses into Parisian life. This guide is different. We don't suggest that you completely shun the Louvre or the Orangerie for edgy coffee shops and far-flung *quartiers*. Instead, adopt the Parisian pace of life, finding a balance between the mainstream and offbeat sights. Leave plenty of time for the good things in life: eating, drinking, and simply soaking up your surroundings.

This book has been curated to guide you to the city's lesser-known highlights, from unusual artworks in the most-visited galleries to overlooked museums, secret squares, and parks where tourists rarely venture. You won't find snooty bistros or international chains here. Instead, expect local favorites: casual neighborhood spots, standing-room-only wine bars, and quirky boutique hotels. If somewhere isn't really worth visiting, even though it's conveniently located or endlessly over-hyped, you won't find it included here.

To help you get the most from your trip, we've trawled the racks at the city's best consignment stores, sipped espressos (and even the odd matcha latte) at the most-talked-about cafés, and covered ourselves in crumbs while rigorously taste-testing the best croissants. Throughout this guide you'll find the local insights we've gleaned along the way. What should you *really* order at apéro hour? What souvenirs are actually worth buying? And how do you begin to choose from the myriad pâtisseries on display in practically every street-corner bakery?

In short, we want to make a city that's renowned for being aloof approachable. This is an insider's guide without pretension.

INTRODUCTION

Simply put, Paris is Europe's most magical capital. Every cliché about the city rings true. The Eiffel Tower really does provide a glittering backdrop to sunset picnics along the Seine; the sidewalk cafés are every bit as photogenic as you'd expect; the diversity of the museums and galleries is astounding; and you'll stumble upon a secret garden, monument, or architectural marvel at seemingly every turn. There's a reason why this is the most visited city in the world.

A week here can easily be passed in a dreamlike haze, hopping between galleries and museums, snapping photos, and seeking out views. Days become punctuated by the boulangerie line at breakfast, choosing the best sunny café for lunch, and settling in for three-hour dinners at night. After dark, you can trace the footsteps of film stars and literary heroes in the city's cabarets and cocktail bars. Few other places have played such an important role in the development of modern art and culture. Literary greats including Molière, Honoré de Balzac, Victor Hugo, and Marcel Proust all called the city home. In the Roaring '20s, this is where the luminaries of the so-called lost generation—including Gertrude Stein, Ernest Hemingway, F. Scott Fitzgerald, and Ford Madox Ford—wrote some of their most famous works. Cubism was founded here by Pablo Picasso and Georges Braque. Every form of music has flourished in the city, from classical, jazz, and rap to Édith Piaf's haunting ballads.

But if you come to Paris for a storybook trip alone, you're seriously missing out. Give yourself the chance to fall in love with Parisian life for what it really is; the experience will be richer and more memorable than what any tour could provide.

Paris isn't as picture-perfect as most travel guides would have you believe. Like all great cities, it's loud, busy, and a little bit gritty. In the past few years, it's also undergone a huge transformation. Once down-at-heel quartiers are now peppered with independent boutiques, specialty coffee shops, and secret speakeasies. A love affair with upscale fine dining has been replaced by one with cool-yet-casual bistros and new wave wine bars. Modern art isn't confined to galleries but is expressed through fashion, graffiti, and tattoos. The city's nightlife flourishes in clubs and at pop-up parties, while that freedom is curtailed in other European capitals in the face of regulation. And pioneering redevelopment projects are gradually pedestrianizing much of the city center, with a view to making Paris one of the world's greenest capitals.

You won't find romance in the obvious places, but in the everyday: getting utterly lost in the backstreets of Montmartre, hopping down an art deco entrance to the métro, finding a designer treasure at a flea market, deciphering a perplexing handwritten restaurant menu, or bagging a pair of rusty chairs to soak up the sun in the Jardin des Tuileries. The joy of visiting Paris isn't in seeing the big sights, but in discovering a little bit of Parisian life for yourself.

FIND YOUR WAY AROUND

P aris is a relatively small city, divided into 20 arrondissements that spiral out from the Seine river in a snail-like curl. At the center are two islands, Île Saint-Louis and Île de la Cité, where the city was first settled and Notre-Dame Cathedral built. The most famous landmarks—and consequently the largest numbers of tourists—are found along the river, while many major museums and galleries lie along the stretch running from the Louvre toward the Champs-Élysées.

North of the river, known as the Right Bank, is the city's heart and commercial center. Yet each neighborhood retains a distinct character, from historic spots like the Marais's boutique-filled lanes and the galleried

CLOCKWISE FROM TOP LEFT: THE VIEW FROM THE ARC DE TRIOMPHE; THE PALAIS ROYAL; THE VIEW FROM THE SACRÉ-CŒUR; SQUARE DU VERT-GALANT, ILE DE LA CITÉ

passages that intersect the city's classical boulevards to areas like Sentier that are being transformed by hip hotels and cocktail bars. You'll find the best views over the Right Bank's myriad quartiers from the basilica of the Sacré-Cœur, which is the crowning glory of hilltop Montmartre. Beneath it, Pigalle and SoPi are shaking off their once seedy reputations and becoming some of the best spots for nightlife and dining.

The Left Bank, south of the river, might have been bohemian in Hemingway's day but is now smart and refined—and is generally known for being the most expensive part of Paris. Great art museums rub shoulders with

ALL ABOUT ARRONDISSEMENTS

Speak to a Parisian and they won't tell you the name of their neighborhood but the number of their arrondissement. The city is divided into 20 arrondissements—all of which are packed inside the *périphérique* (the city's ring road) within an area barely 6 miles across. Each has its own distinct identity and reputation. Snobbery abounds. Some claim the chichi 8th is the only place to live, others declare it boring and staid. The laid-back vibe of 11th makes it the most exciting district for many; its critics find it grimy. Paying a premium to have a different number at the end of an address is commonplace, as is fiercely defending the merits of your chosen quartier.

Stay for a while, and you'll quickly form your own opinions. But if you're only on a short visit, don't worry too much about memorizing the intricacies of the system. We've included arrondissements for all sights, restaurants, and hotels in this guide so you can easily ask for directions to check that you're following the right route. You'll see arrondissements written in shorthand (such as 1er, 10ème, or 15e) as well as in zip code format (75001, 75010, 75015). Roman numerals also crop up occasionally, mostly for the 10th (Xème) or 20th (XXème).

CLOCKWISE FROM TOP LEFT: ARCHITECTURE IN THE MARAIS; RUE BERTHE; RUE CREMIEUX; CROSSING THE CANAL SAINT-MARTIN

high fashion in Saint-Germain, while the Jardin du Luxembourg remains the most genteel green space for a stroll. In the Latin Quarter, you can trace the city's revolutionary student history, or step back in time with a visit to the city's few remaining Roman ruins. Head farther south and you'll find yourself in a swathe of peaceful residential districts, dotted by a couple of unusual sights.

Paris's eastern arrondissements are the most exciting. The Canal Saint-Martin is the hub of the action, from where numerous restaurants, bars, and clubs spill east into the 10th and 11th arrondissements. This is definitely not tourist territory and one of the most laid-back parts of the city. Visit there to search for the latest culinary superstars and to wander through diverse neighborhoods like Belleville.

EATING AND DRINKING

Food should be central to any trip to Paris. Whether your idea of heaven is biting into a smushy cream-filled éclair or sitting down for one of the city's top multicourse menus, French gastronomy is sure to amaze. The city's food culture thrives everywhere you look, from the local markets that take place weekly in each arrondissement, to the boulangeries, épiceries, and boucheries where everyone shops for specialty ingredients that are simply *unthinkable* to get from a supermarket.

The ritual of sitting down to eat is held sacred by the French. Coffees are generally drunk at a table, not from a to-go cup; many people still take a full hour for lunch during the week (if not a little more); and long, lazy, late dinners are the norm. Parisian restaurants are simply some of the best in the world. But that's not to say you should start popping champagne corks and looking for your credit card. Thanks to the bistronomy movement, some of the city's best chefs no longer cook in gilded hotel dining rooms but at informal and affordable bistros, free from traditional trappings like white tablecloths and haughty sommeliers. Tasting menus abound, but they might draw influences from Asia or Scandinavia, and

CLOCKWISE FROM TOP LEFT: LA ROSE DE FRANCE; BRASSERIE LES DEUX PALAIS; THE PARIS-BREST AT BISTROT PAUL BERT; CHOUX PUFFS FROM POPELINI

will almost certainly favor local and seasonal produce over luxuries like caviar and cognac.

Classic bistros have also made a comeback of late, dishing up hearty *plats* (entrées) like boeuf bourguignon and confit de canard accompanied by cheap carafes of wine. Price-conscious but discerning diners will pack out anywhere with artfully distressed deco features and mirror-backed bars—and coq au vin and steak-frites certainly aren't just served to visitors. Lunch can be a particularly good time to eat out, as you can usually get a *formule* (a set menu of two or three courses), for much less than the same dishes would cost you at dinner.

Even for street food, you'll be spoiled for choice. Nutella-filled crêpes and galettes oozing melted cheese just beg to be sampled, as do chestnuts roasted on outdoor braziers in winter. You should also check out the city's more cosmopolitan highlights: tahini-drizzled falafel wraps made at hole-in-the-wall takeout joints; authentic Vietnamese kitchens that make fantastic pho and little more; and gelaterias where you can buy pistachio-crusted Middle Eastern–style ice-cream cones.

Parisian pâtisserie is in a class of its own. The finest pâtissiers turn out creations that are closer to artworks than teatime treats. You'll see macarons and cream puff-like choux buns everywhere you go, as well as beautiful *tarts au citron* and *tarts au chocolat* (lemon and chocolate tarts). Even local boulangeries will have a shelf of millefeuilles and religieuses. Just remember that pâtisserie is considered a separate discipline to baking. For the best of the best you'll need to make a pilgrimage to the solo-owned shops of big-name pâtissiers, the rock stars of the current culinary world with the fan clubs to match.

The only time Paris can be a let down is when it comes to vegetarian cuisine. Even so, the range of options is gradually starting to expand as the city embraces new ideas: brunch, vegan cafés, juice bars, and even the odd gluten-free bakery.

Jambon-beurre. Sandwiches simply don't get more satisfying than baguettes liberally spread with butter and stuffed with thick-cut slices of ham.

Pain au chocolat. Many judge boulangeries on their croissants, but a delicate and flaky pain au chocolat is often the better arbiter of a baker's skill.

Steak-frites. Preferably with the steak served *saignant* (rare) and accompanied by perfectly crispy fries.

Croque-monsieur. Essentially a grilled cheese sandwich filled with ham and topped with béchamel, usually served with a green salad on the side.

Macarons. Picking the right rainbow-colored macarons can make or break a picnic; you can never go wrong with salted caramel or raspberry.

Paris-Brest. A wheel-shaped confection of choux pastry filled with praline cream created to celebrate the inaugural Paris–Brest cycle race in 1910.

Confit de canard. This dish of duck legs slow-cooked in fat might hail from southwest France, but it's a Parisian bistro staple.

Cheese. Whether you order a fromage platter with a glass of wine or a cheese course, you can't come to Paris without getting stuck into a slice of stinky époisses or nutty comté.

Éclairs. Choose from a dizzying range of flavors, from classics like chocolate and coffee to passion fruit and blood orange.

Poulet rôti. Roasted chickens spin on spits across the city; they might not be a gourmet triumph, but they're the ultimate comfort food.

SIGHTSEEING

Museums with global reputations come with the lines to match, so it pays to do your research. One of the best ways to beat the crowds is to check out late openings; most museums stay open until 9 p.m. or 10 p.m. one night a week. If you plan to visit more than a handful of the big hitters, you should also think about investing in a Paris Museum Pass, both to save on ticket costs and to take advantage of fast-track entry. That said, offbeat museums are the city's specialty. Galleries dedicated to single artists abound, as do esoteric collections celebrating everything from hunting trophies to fairground rides. You could quite easily miss all of the famous names, and instead get caught up in thought-provoking photography exhibits at the Jeu de Paume, stepping back to medieval Paris at the Musée de Cluny, or spend an enchanting hour at the Musée de la Vie Romantique.

There's also plenty to marvel at outdoors. The architecture of many monuments and churches is more impressive from the exterior than from within, and you should dedicate at least half a day to just strolling the Seine and appreciating the vistas. Fountain-filled parks and gardens are free to explore, and a picnic outdoors in place des Vosges or Parc des Buttes-Chaumont might just be the highlight of your trip. Elsewhere in the city, the street art scene in Paris is booming, with artworks even commissioned by the *Mairie* (the city government).

There's just one rule to remember: bring comfy shoes. Paris is a city best explored on foot.

SHOPPING

Parisian style is hard to pinpoint. Is it the tousled hair that makes everyone look so effortlessly chic? Is it the generally adopted wardrobe of muted blacks and grays? Is it the perfectly tied scarves that Parisians seem to pull off so well? You'll quickly form your own opinions—and

CLOCKWISE FROM TOP LEFT: PASSAGE VERDEAU; GALLERIES LAFAYETTE; ASTIER DE VILLATTE

you'll find an abundance of boutiques, department stores, and treasure-trove *dépôts-vente* (high-end consignment and vintage stores) to support you in your pursuit of sartorial perfection.

Quality and individuality are highly prized everywhere you look, from the storefronts of designer labels to cute cut-price boutiques. The same is true for beautifully made basics like tees, jeans, and sleepwear. In general, the city's style is becoming more casual, focused on streetwear rather than stilettos. Favored designers change regularly. Brands like Sézane have been transformed overnight from online sensations to household names—and while Dior and Chanel accessories will never go out of style, affordable cool-kid labels like Rouje, Maje, A.P.C., and IRO are the most coveted.

Even window shopping in Paris can be a joy. The great department stores of Printemps, Le Bon Marché, and Galeries Lafayette are architectural wonders in their own right, as are the city's covered arcades, known as *passages*. For luxury, you can't beat pressing your nose against the windows of the great fashion houses in the so-called Golden Triangle, which connects avenue Montaigne, rue Saint-Honoré, and Place Vendôme, the latter renowned for glittering, gorgeous, and completely unaffordable jewelry. More practical areas to shop include the Marais—peppered with tiny one-of-a-kind accessories and interiors stores—and Saint-Germain, which is expensive but in parts still accessible.

For many, however, the pinnacle of Parisian shopping is beauty products. Even pharmacies are celebrated for their ranges of quality skin and hair care, including cult brands like Caudalie, La Roche-Posay, Bioderma, Klorane, and Avène. If you're into fragrance, colognes and perfumes make great gifts—as do scented candles, which no Parisian home is without.

Bargains are best found at flea markets, particularly Les Puces de Saint-Ouen to the north of the city and the Marché aux Puces de Vanves to the south. Amid the bric-a-brac you'll spot antique tableware, artwork, books, records, and the occasional smattering of vintage designer clothing.

NIGHTLIFE

Paris stays up late. On a Friday or Saturday night you can happily sit down to dinner after 9 p.m., then go for a drink around midnight. Most bars are open until at least two or three, and many keep their terrasses heated so you can sit outside well into the early hours. Evenings pass at a relaxed pace with table service, tunes, and a good deal of chain smoking. Cocktail culture has developed more slowly, but the city's now making up for lost time. From Belleville to Pigalle, mixology is suddenly being taken much more seriously—and French spirits are seeing something of a renaissance.

You can find all-night partying if you go looking for it, too, both in the center of Paris at club-and-event spaces like La Bellevilloise and dance music–centric clubs that float along the Seine. One-off pop-up parties and DJs are best discovered on social media and sites like Resident Advisor; although the best may take you to somewhat sketchy neighborhoods outside the périphérique. Even more memorable is a night at a jazz bar or a Parisian cabaret—but eschew any ideas of high kicks and ruffled petticoats and head instead for the shocking yet sophisticated shows at the Crazy Horse.

ITINERARIES

PARIS IN TWO DAYS

If you've only got two days in Paris, don't try to pack in too much. Book a hotel in the center of the city and prioritize exploring on foot and some special meals as well as big sights and great museums.

▶ DAY 1

Morning: Get your bearings in the Marais, one of the oldest and most enchanting quartiers. Walk through stately place des Vosges, where Victor Hugo once lived, before browsing the Marché des Enfants Rouges, the first market in the city.

Lunch: Sip a glass of rosé and order a croque-madame with a green salad at Haut Marais stalwart Cafe Charlot, a classic order at a classic Parisian pavement café.

Afternoon: Pick up a cappuccino to go from bijou coffee shop Yellow Tucan and hit the river. Early afternoon is the perfect time to stroll the banks of the Seine, slowly idling your way past Île de la Cité and the famous *bouquinistes* (booksellers). It'll take you around 45 minutes to reach the magnificent Musée d'Orsay, where you can spend the rest of the day getting lost in the works of great Impressionist painters.

Evening: As dusk falls, cross the river to visit the Jardin des Tuileries, ending up at the Louvre's famous pyramid at the gardens' eastern end, which is often bathed in golden light as the sun sets. Save the museum's collections for another trip.

Dinner: Book a table at Le Mermoz, just off the Champs-Élysées, for a taste of the city's new approach to gourmet dining: bare tables, small plates, and friendly wine-bar-style service in the evening.

Night: Fall down a cabaret rabbit hole and catch one of the risqué late-night shows at the Crazy Horse. Expect sophisticated nudity—and plenty of champagne.

▶ DAY 2

Breakfast: Grab a pain au chocolat or sweet pastry escargot from cult bakery Du Pain et des Idées to eat by the graffiti-lined Canal Saint-Martin.

Morning: After browsing the canal-side boutiques make your way toward the Atelier des Lumières, billed as the world's first digital fine-art museum. Designed to display great masters' work with an experiential twist, it's unlike any gallery you'll have visited before.

Lunch: You're near some of the city's best restaurants so make the most of lunchtime formules. Le Servan and Tannat epitomize the laid-back bistronomy movement, and offer great-value two- and three-course menus that cost a fraction of what you'd pay in the evening.

Afternoon: Take the métro to Montmartre where you can walk off your lunch climbing the 300 or so steps to the Sacré-Cœur. Be sure to leave time to tour the peaceful basilica before you rest your legs at the top of the butte and take in the superb views over the city. If you've got time, seek out the tiny vineyard hidden just to the north.

Dinner: Go old school for dinner at Bouillon Pigalle, the brasserie reinvented. From snails and steak-frites to éclairs and profiteroles, the menu is full of textbook French classics.

Night: If you've still got energy, you'll find plenty of spots for a nightcap on rue Frochot, where American-inspired cocktail bars like Glass mix with Parisian originals like Les Justes.

CLOCKWISE FROM THE TOP: PONT ALEXANDRE III; DU PAIN ET DES IDÉES; SACRÉ-CŒUR

PARIS ON A BUDGET

Paris's reputation as an expensive city is in many ways unfounded. It's easy to eat extremely well for very little, and there are plenty of free sights to explore. While most museums charge a small entry fee, some of the most famous sights are free to visit, including the most magnificent parks and gardens.

Breakfast: A pain au chocolat should never cost you more than €1.50, but it's the most delicious way to start the day. Get to Boulangerie Utopie before 9 a.m. and you'll be served pastries still warm from the oven.

Morning: Mix classical architecture with counter-cultural art by exploring 59 Rivoli, a graffiti-covered gallery meets squat on the edge of the Marais. It's just a short walk onward to the gardens of the Palais Royal, one of the city's loveliest spots to stroll, surrounded by elegant colonnades.

Lunch: For less than €20 you can have a filling lunch of steak or roast chicken at delightfully old-fashioned Bistrot Victoires—plus crème brûlée for dessert.

Afternoon: Stop off at Atelier Brancusi, one of the city's few free galleries, to learn more about the life and work of the fascinating sculptor. You can also pay your respects to other great artists who called Paris home: A short métro ride east to the fascinating Cimetière du Père Lachaise will take you to the final resting place of luminaries such as Oscar Wilde and Jim Morrison.

Dinner: Budget dining doesn't mean bad dining. Start with a delicious glass of natural wine for around €5 at the locals' spot Café du Coin, and order a gourmet pizzette and salad to snack on. You can even stop for a drink and a snack at Septime La Cave, the affordable tiny wine bar of the city's coolest Michelin-star restaurant.

Night: If the night still feels young, head to La Bellevilloise for lineups that range from jazz and funk to cumbia and hip hop. Tickets are around €20, which is great value for a night at this superb arts venue meets club.

CLOCKWISE FROM TOP LEFT: CAFÉ DU COIN; PEEKING THROUGH DOORWAYS IN THE MARAIS; SUNSET NEAR THE MARAIS; A WEEKLY MARKET IN THE 9TH

You could spend months living in Paris and barely scratch the surface of the city's culinary culture. So, if you've only got a day or so to dedicate to epicurean delights, here are a handful of essential experiences you should try.

Breakfast: La Fontaine de Belleville might look like a classic corner café, but appearances can be misleading. Impeccable sourcing of ingredients elevates even a simple breakfast to new heights. Order an espresso made with their own Belleville Brûlerie beans and a tartine (fresh baguette served with butter and jam).

Morning: Wander south to the Marché d'Aligre, the city's buzziest food market, which will be in full swing by midmorning. Duck into the cheese shops and *traiteurs* (delis) that line the market's ever-growing sprawl before stopping at old-school wine bar Le Baron Rouge for a glass of wine .

Lunch: After a morning on your feet, you should have worked up an appetite. Bag a table at Clamato for a seafood feast—perhaps Breton oysters followed by a Peruvian-inspired ceviche. Just be prepared to wait for a table.

Afternoon: Head for the Marais for dessert. Stop by Maison Aleph for Levantine pâtisserie reimagined using French techniques, or go to L'Eclair de Génie to sample their latest éclair fillings, perhaps pistachio and raspberry or apricot cheesecake.

Evening: Cross the river, stopping for a sorbet at the city's most famous ice-cream shop Berthillon, on your way to Saint-Germain. Yves Camdeborde was one of the first to popularize the concept of casual bistronomy at his standing-room-only tapas bar, L'Avant Comptoir de la Terre, where you can stop for an apéro and a bite to eat.

Dinner: Still got room for dinner proper? Head to Fish La Boissonnerie to explore one of the most exciting wine lists in the city with an inventive three-course dinner; despite the name, fish is not the focus.

Night: Finish the night with cocktails (or mocktails, if it's all getting a bit much) at Prescription Cocktail Club, the best speakeasy south of the Seine.

PARIS FOR SOLO TRAVELERS

Paris is a solo traveler's dream. Sidewalk cafés are often best enjoyed alone, and you're spoiled for choice when it comes to museums and galleries. If you're feeling sociable, simply book yourself onto a tour or draw up a stool for a cocktail.

Breakfast: The key to traveling solo is starting with plenty of fuel for the day. Pancakes and a strong coffee at buzzy Coutume Café will get you ready to hit the streets.

Morning: Book onto a movie-themed walking tour with Set in Paris, which will bring the Left Bank and the islands to life through your favorite on-screen moments. Then set out solo to explore two of Saint-Germain's most peaceful spots: the Jardin du Luxembourg and the Musée Rodin.

Lunch: Cross the river to the cutting-edge contemporary art gallery, Palais de Tokyo. Before you explore the latest installations, stop for lunch at Les Grands Verres—this gallery restaurant with a difference is a super spot for dining alone with plenty of bar seats.

Afternoon: Once you've had enough art appreciation for the day, stroll past the glitzy high-fashion stores on avenue Montaigne before embracing the greatest Parisian tradition, sitting en terrasse outside a classic corner café. Late afternoon is prime people-watching time, so choose your coffee spot wisely. At Le Musset, you get both chic shoppers from rue Saint-Honoré and tourists pouring into the Louvre.

Dinner: Pull up a bar seat for dinner at Charles Compagnon's sleek neo-bistro, Le 52, designed with drop-in-drop-out all-day dining in mind. You could find yourself trying anything from an unusual bouillabaisse foam to a seemingly traditional duck breast with confit shallots.

Night: If you're not sure about bar hopping alone, check out the late shows at the glorious art deco cinema, Le Grand Rex.

CLOCKWISE FROM THE TOP: THE COULÉE
VERTE; BRASSERIE GEORGES, CENTRE
POMPIDOU; CAFÉ DE LA NOUVELLE MAIRIE

PARIS OFF THE BEATEN TRACK

There's so much more to discover in Paris than the major galleries and most-talked-about restaurants. From unusual museums and hidden cafés to flea markets on the city's perimeter, these are a few of the lesser-known highlights.

Breakfast: Shun croissants for a day. Head to southeast Paris for a traditional Vietnamese breakfast at Pho Bàhn Cúon 14, where you can slurp noodles in a quartier rarely discovered by tourists.

Morning: You'll need to arrive early to pick up the best bargains at the Marché aux Puces de Vanves, an affordable street-side flea market just to the south of the city. Artwork, Hermès scarves, and tableware are a few of the treasures you might be able to pick up.

Lunch: Settle in for lunch at Café de la Nouvelle Mairie, a weekday-only spot in the Latin Quarter where locals cram in for great wines and the traditional plat du jour.

Afternoon: You might just find medieval Paris unexpectedly fascinating after a visit to the Musée de Cluny. Its historical highlights include the *Lady with the Unicorn*, a series of six tapestries from the 1500s masterfully depicting the five senses—and a sixth sense that remains a mystery. Stop to reflect with mint tea at the nearby courtyard café at the Grande Mosquée de Paris.

Dinner: Cross the river for dinner on the Right Bank. Bonhomie's slick Mediterranean-inspired menu could see you sharing anything from chicken with roasted cauliflower and tabouleh to small plates of falafel and hummus.

Night: Finish up the night with post-dinner cocktails at the cool cocktail bar Le Syndicat, a temple to French spirits behind an unsigned façade on the once-infamous but fast-gentrifying rue du Faubourg Saint-Denis.

Great art is almost everywhere you look in Paris: in the city's architecture, in its galleries, and in its museums. You can't fail to find inspiration at some point, whether your interest is piqued by street art or 18th-century portraits.

Breakfast: A great coffee is an art form in itself. Order an espresso and a cinnamon roll at coffee bar 5 Pailles.

Morning: Make modern art the focus of your morning with a thorough exploration of the extensive collections at the Centre Pompidou, designed by Renzo Piano and Richard Rogers, and now home to masterpieces by the likes of Mondrian, Pollock, and Warhol. If you're feeling energetic, you can also swing by the Musée Picasso before lunch.

Lunch: Enter the Belle Époque for lunch at Poulette, where the zinc bar is backed by pastel tiles painted with Greek goddesses. The features might not be original, but the setting can't be beaten.

Afternoon: Dive into the world of symbolist painter Gustave Moreau at his eponymous museum in Pigalle, which houses nearly 4,000 works by the artist. Afterward, stop for tea and cake in the garden of the tiny Musée de la Vie Romantique round the corner, which offers a rare glimpse into Parisian artistic life in the 1800s.

Dinner: Small plates are everywhere in Paris, but only Ellsworth manages to make mini portions of fried chicken worthy of a spot in your vacation photo album.

Night: Hop aboard a post-dinner Seine cruise to see the city's architecture by night. The Conciergerie is illuminated on the Île de la Cité, and the Eiffel Tower glitters from top to toe every hour.

PARIS OUTDOORS

Whatever the weather, Paris is a city that embraces the outdoors: Games of pétanque take place year-round, and it's never too cold for a stroll along the Coulée Verte. Wrap up warm, or slap on the sunscreen, and embrace days spent in the fresh air.

Breakfast: The outdoor tables at Beans on Fire, on leafy Square Maurice Gardette, are coveted even on the chilliest mornings. Their hot chocolate is worth a try, too.

Morning: It's a steep walk to the top of Parc des Buttes-Chaumont, but from this park, one of the city's least visited but loveliest green spaces, you'll be rewarded with views across to the Sacré-Cœur. Walk on to the Bassin de la Villette to stroll by the water.

Lunch: Your reward for a morning on your feet? Sampling Parisian-brewed beers on the deck at the Paname Brewing Company with one of their signature burgers.

Afternoon: Walk among rooftops along the elevated Coulée Verte, the inspiration for New York's High Line, which runs all the way from Bastille to the Bois de Vincennes on the city's edges. If that sounds a bit ambitious, cross the river for a more sedate stroll along the shady avenues of the Jardin des Plantes.

Dinner: Aux Bons Crus might be indoors, but it re-creates the atmosphere of a country roadside restaurant. The food is classic, filling, and just what you need after a day of exploring.

Night: Step aboard a *péniche* (bar-boat) to end your evening alfresco. A string of club-bars line the river southeast of the Gare d'Austerlitz, or you can stop for a cocktail at the bar of the floating hotel, OFF Seine.

CHAPTER 1

The Louvre to the Champs-Élysées

The sights clustered around the Louvre and along the avenue des Champs-Élysées, stretching west from the 1st arrondissement into the 8th, are the city's big-ticket attractions. This is Paris at its grandest: world-famous museums and stately palaces interspersed by statue-filled gardens, swanky shops, and the city's ritziest hotels. You'd be hard-pressed to find a 3-mile stretch anywhere else in the world so rich with art and culture. Yet despite the crowds, this part of Paris remains utterly majestic. The landmarks here were—quite literally—designed and laid out to be visited on foot. It's an area made for linear exploration, starting in the east at the Louvre and working west toward the Arc de Triomphe or even farther out to the woody Bois de Boulogne.

Deciding whether or not to visit the Louvre itself is a tricky question. Its collections might be unrivaled, stretching from antiquities to art (most notably, the Mona Lisa), but the lines can be epic. You won't be disappointed if you just come to admire the exterior and the beautiful courtyard; American architect I. M. Pei's modern glass pyramid divided the critics when it was built over the museum's entrance in 1989, but today few structures are as synonymous with the city. If you do decide to descend the famous escalators, plan ahead to make the most of your time and seek out little-visited wings to escape the crowds.

Nearby, the courtyard garden of the Palais Royal often gets overlooked in favor of better-known sights, but it's a welcome oasis from the crowds. A stroll through the shady arcades of the formal Jardin des Tuileries is also de rigueur, its elm and mulberry trees offering dappled shade in summer. It's here that you'll find the Orangerie, which houses Monet's ethereal masterpieces depicting his Japanese garden and water lily pond, and contemporary photography gallery, the Jeu de Paume. They stand in contrast to the traffic-choked place de la Concorde at the gardens' western end. This uniquely French landmark is part road intersection part public square. It's most famous for the 75-foot Egyptian obelisk that stands at its center and its grisly history as the site of Louis XVI and Marie Antoinette's executions by guillotine during the French revolution. The neighboring

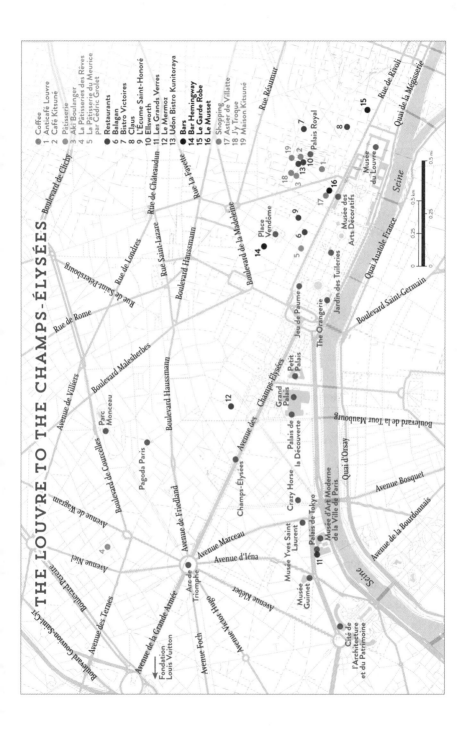

THE LOUVRE TO THE CHAMPS-ÉLYSÉES

Coffee
1 Anticafé Louvre
2 Café Kitsuné

Pâtisserie
3 Aki Boulanger
4 La Pâtisserie des Rêves
5 La Pâtisserie du Meurice par Cédric Grolet

Restaurants
6 Balagan
7 Bistro Victoires
8 Claus
9 L'Écume Saint-Honoré
10 Ellsworth
11 Les Grands Verres
12 Le Mermoz
13 Udon Bistro Kunitoraya

Bars
14 Bar Hemingway
15 Le Garde Robe
16 Le Musset

Shopping
17 Astier de Villatte
18 J'y Troque
19 Maison Kitsuné

Grand Palais and Petit Palais, meanwhile, are confusingly not palaces but purpose-built exhibition spaces on a monumental scale.

You'll notice a marked change in atmosphere as you reach the Champs-Élysées, once considered Europe's most elegant avenue, leading up to the Arc de Triomphe (worth climbing if you don't mind narrow staircases). Today, chain stores dominate: Locals don't shop here, and neither should you. For those with serious cash to splash, however, there's a different side of the Champs-Élysées to discover in the so-called Golden Triangle. Rue Saint-Honoré is the most prestigious address for luxury boutiques, while Coco Chanel's one-time home on Place Vendôme (she decadently lived in a suite at the Ritz for more than 30 years) is the place to press your nose against the windows of jewelry brands like Cartier and Van Cleef & Arpels. Many of the grandes dames of the five-star hotel scene are also found around here; even if you don't stay, you can visit for a round of cocktails or a blowout afternoon tea.

You should also head off the well-trodden routes in search of smaller sights. The Musée Yves Saint Laurent is one of the highest-profile openings of the last few years, a compact collection of the designer's work showcased in his old atelier. Modern art lovers should check out the paintings at the Musée d'Art Moderne de la Ville de Paris and venture beyond the périphérique for the latest slick international exhibition at the Fondation Louis Vuitton. At the other end of the spectrum are the exhibitions at the Palais de Tokyo, possibly the city's most challenging contemporary art space known for pushing boundaries—and critics' buttons.

When you've reached your culture threshold, some of the surrounding chichi residential neighborhoods are interesting to wander, as is Parc Monceau, one of the smartest parks in the city and one of the best spots to admire the cherry blossom in spring. The only downside to this part of Paris is that the proliferation of fancy hotels can make it feel a little soulless. Counteract this by eating and drinking in local spots: cool cafés or authentic udon joints in Little Tokyo. After the sun goes down, there's the city's most risqué cabaret show at the Crazy Horse to discover.

CLOCKWISE FROM TOP LEFT: THE VIEW FROM THE ARC DE TRIOMPHE; THE VIEW FROM THE ROOF AT THE
FONDATION LOUIS VUITTON; CAROUSEL IN THE JARDIN DES TUILERIES

SEE

Musée du Louvre

Rue de Rivoli, 1st
Closed Tuesday
louvre.fr

The Louvre defies comprehension. Opened in 1793, it's home to a simply astonishing array of paintings, sculpture, and objets d'art. Its eight collections, which are spread over three wings, are visited by nearly 10 million people a year. You simply can't see it all, even in a day. If you do decide to visit, think carefully about what you want to see—and if that's the Mona Lisa, you'd better be prepared to battle vast crowds just to get a glimpse. You may find lesser-visited galleries, such as the collection of Islamic arts, opened in 2012, more appealing. Whichever part of the museum you choose to explore, pick up an audio guide or book a tour, otherwise you'll leave with little more than superficial insights. The other secret to getting the most from your visit is to avoid the lines: Late opening on Wednesdays and Fridays will give you more time to explore. Check out Five Tips for Beating the Crowds on page 42.

Musée des Arts Décoratifs

107 rue de Rivoli, 1st
Closed Monday
madparis.fr

While it's housed in a wing of the Louvre, the Musée des Arts Décoratifs is a separate museum dedicated to French craftsmanship. It holds an astonishing 150,000 objets d'art—although only a fraction of those will be on display at any one time. Depending on your interests, you can trace the development of ceramics and furniture from the Middle Ages to the 20th century, discover more about art nouveau and art deco, or explore kitchen designs for Le Corbusier's controversial Unité d'Habitation in Marseille. It may not be part of the Louvre proper, but its proximity means it still attracts plenty of crowds, so don't expect to browse in peace.

Jardin des Tuileries

1st

Whether you stroll the dusty avenues in spring or wander beneath burnished copper leaves in the fall, the Jardin des Tuileries never fails to enchant. Manet, Pissarro, and Monet are among the artists who painted here en plein air, while more recently the gardens have even provided the backdrop for Chanel fashion shoots. The garden's formal layout was designed by André Le Nôtre, the visionary responsible for the majestic grounds of Versailles, who created them from a site once home to the city's *tuileries* (tile factories), hence the name. Grass is thin on the ground; instead, chestnut groves, statues, and meticulously maintained hedges and flowerbeds intersect wide and straight paths. On warm days, do as the locals do and fight for one of the famous green metal chairs around the glassy pond at the gardens' western end.

The Orangerie

Jardin des Tuileries, 1st
Closed Tuesday
musee-orangerie.fr

For a small museum, the Orangerie packs an emotional punch. For many, it holds the city's most special art collection. Originally built as a shelter for the Tuileries' orange trees in the 19th century, the building was converted to house Claude Monet's mesmerizing water lily series, *Les Nymphéas,* which he donated to the state as a symbol for peace to mark the Armistice on November 11, 1918. The gallery was designed under the artist's own guidance and opened in 1927, one year after his death. Today, several rounds of renovations later, two oval rooms immerse you in his ethereal waterscapes, their power amplified by stark white walls. Downstairs you'll find the Jean Walter and Paul Guillaume collection, Impressionist works by the likes of Cézanne, Matisse, and Renoir, as well as temporary exhibitions.

In the world's most visited city, you should come prepared to encounter crowds at the big sights—but there are a few tips and tricks that can help you beat the worst of the lines.

Invest in a Paris Museum Pass

It's good to be skeptical of all-in-one passes, but this one really can be worth the money. From around €50 for two days you get free entry to most of the big museums and fast-track entry at those with the worst lines: the Louvre, Musée d'Orsay, and Centre Pompidou. You can buy it in advance and have it shipped (en.parismuseumpass.com), or you can pick one up in Paris.

Go late

Most museums offer late opening until around 10 p.m. one or two nights a week. Turn up at 6 p.m. and you'll find you've got time for a much more peaceful visit before sitting down to a late dinner. Many Parisians don't eat until around 9 p.m., so you shouldn't have a problem getting a table.

Pick your exhibits carefully

Many of the city's big museums are, well, seriously big. Yet visitors tend to cluster in specific wings, waiting in line to take a picture of a painting or statue they've seen reproduced hundreds of times before. You're likely to have a more memorable experience if you head off in a different direction in search of something new.

Book a tour

If you've got some cash to flash, consider booking an expert-led small group tour. Paris Muse (parismuse.com) offers some of the best, including bespoke tours set up for those with little ones in tow, and some of their guides are educated to masters or doctorate level in their subject.

Don't eat in the obvious places

The quickest way to develop sightseeing ennui is to leave a gallery and go straight into a café packed with a ton of other people dissecting their experience. Make the effort to go a little farther away from the obvious spots and you'll be rewarded both by the quality of the food and the relative calm.

Jeu de Paume

1 place de la Concorde, 8th

Closed Monday

jeudepaume.org

With the Orangerie just a few hundred meters away on the other side of the Jardin de Tuileries, many visitors miss its mirror image entirely. That's a shame, as the Jeu de Paume holds some of the city's top contemporary photography and video exhibitions, with past shows including work by the likes of Ai Weiwei, Martin Parr, and Cindy Sherman. The topics covered are often challenging and political with shows changing every few months; check what's on before you go. The building was originally a court used for real tennis (the precursor to the modern sport), and a lot is packed into a small space: two floors of galleries with a surprisingly good Japanese café in between.

Palais Royal

8 rue de Montpensier, 1st

Historic architecture and contemporary design coexist surprisingly happily in Paris—but few places strike a balance like the Palais Royal. Once a royal residence, before Versailles was built outside the city, the palace has been converted into municipal buildings. But its beautiful garden is free to explore; it's at its loveliest when its flowerbeds burst into bloom in the spring. More often photographed is the palace's grand courtyard, home to two superb modern art installations commissioned by the Ministry of Culture in 1985: the Sphérades, bubbling silver-sphere fountains by Belgian artist Pol Bury; and the Colonnes de Buren, 260 black-and-white-striped octagonal columns, many of which you can climb to strike your best pose. Once controversial, they're now much loved complements to the Palais Royal's elegant arcades.

THE PALAIS ROYAL

Place Vendôme

1st

This astonishingly grandiose square is the spiritual center of luxury in Paris. Coco Chanel lived here in a suite at the Ritz for more than 30 years—and it's said she even designed the first Chanel N°5 bottle to mirror its proportions. Today, it's still distinguished by the soaring burnished-bronze column at its center, built by Napoleon from enemy cannons, but

PLACE VENDÔME

most visitors' attention is lavished on its jewelry boutiques, including Van Cleef & Arpels, Chopard, Piaget, and more. If you've got a couple of hundred euros to spare, you can even book onto a three-hour course at L'École Van Cleef & Arpels to learn more about gemstones, jewelers' techniques, or enameling.

THE GRAND PALAIS

Grand Palais

3 avenue du Général Eisenhower, 8th
Hours vary depending on exhibitions
grandpalais.fr

Built in 1900 for the Exposition Universelle, the Grand Palais is the largest ironwork and glass structure in the world, its soaring conservatory-style roof instantly recognizable and visible from many points across the city. Inside, its majestic art nouveau domes are divided by green iron arches that soar 45 meters above the enormous atrium. It's a spectacular exhibition space, used for everything from FIAC (the city's contemporary art fair) to fashion week runway shows and blockbuster exhibitions covering the diverse artistry of everyone from Miró to Michael Jackson. There's little reason to come unless you're seeing a show, but those staged here are well worth the advance planning. Just note that most of the Grand Palais is due to be closed from late 2020 to spring 2023 while it undergoes a landmark renovation project.

Palais de la Découverte

Avenue Franklin Delano Roosevelt, 8th
Closed Monday
palais-decouverte.fr

One for kids (and perhaps big kids, too) is the city's science museum, tucked behind and connected to the Grand Palais, although very different in style. It's not really on the same scale as similar museums in London and New York, and in places it is short of information for English speakers, but it'll keep curious minds occupied for at least an hour or so on a rainy day. The museum currently covers a wide range of topics, from chemistry and astrophysics to biology, with additional exhibitions on contemporary topics like robotics or the history of the internet. Along with the Grand Palais, however, it will close from late 2020 for renovations.

Petit Palais

Avenue Winston Churchill, 8th
Closed Monday
petitpalais.paris.fr

The Grand Palais's smaller and slightly stocky cousin, across avenue Winston Churchill, was built at the same time. Its domes are tiled rather than glass but it's still elegant, and even hides a small semicircular garden at its center. While known to all as the Petit Palais, the collections here technically comprise the Musée des Beaux-Arts de la Ville de Paris, which began life as a collection of French art focused on paintings from the late 19th to early 20th century but has since expanded to include objets d'art and sculptures dating back to ancient Greece. While this includes works by the likes of Courbet, Monet, Delacroix, and Gauguin, the real reason to come is the museum's temporary exhibitions. These examine everything from artistic styles and themes to retrospectives dedicated to great figures outside the conventional artistic community, such as Yves Saint Laurent and Oscar Wilde.

Champs-Élysées

Once the city's most prestigious shopping destination, today the Champs-Élysées has rather lost its cachet—although this has done little to dent the street's enduring popularity among tourists. If anyone tells you this is where locals love to shop, a subtle Parisian raise of the eyebrow is definitely in order. Global chains including Sephora, H&M, Abercrombie & Fitch, McDonald's, and Five Guys dominate the mix along with street performers and overpriced and unexciting restaurants. True luxury brands cluster along avenue Montaigne, where you'll need to look like a serious buyer just to cross the threshold.

Arc de Triomphe

Place Charles de Gaulle, 8th
Open daily
paris-arc-de-triomphe.fr

At the center of Place Charles de Gaulle, also known as the Place de l'Étoile for the star-like fan of roads that branch off in every direction, sits the Arc de Triomphe. Its architect, Jean-François Chalgrin, took inspiration from Rome's Arch of Titus and went on to create a monument even larger and grander than the original. Its roof offers simply glorious panoramas of the city, which are well worth the cramped, steep climb and entrance fee. Exhibitions on the arch's history and military uniforms on the way up are less absorbing, but you should make time to pay your respects at the Tomb of the Unknown Soldier at the base of the monument. The flame of remembrance is rekindled here each day at 6:30 p.m.

Parc Monceau

35 boulevard de Courcelles, 8th

In complete contrast to the neat lines and ceremonial layout of the Jardin des Tuileries, Parc Monceau's shady lawns and rose gardens are just the antidote if you're suffering from shopping or sightseeing overload. The park sits in of one of the city's smartest residential areas and is popular with locals who come to flop on the grass with a book or take their kids for a ride on the carousel. As you wander its winding paths, you'll spot several follies scattered throughout the park. Built in the 1700 and 1800s, these include Roman columns improbably backing a duck pond, a Venetian-style bridge, a stone pyramid, and a small Renaissance arch.

Pagoda Paris

48 rue de Courcelles, 8th

Paris is full of surprises, but none are quite as unexpected as this magnificent Chinese pagoda—the same height as the Haussmannian buildings that surround it—just a short stumble from Parc Monceau. Looking at its deep ochre-red exterior, curving tile roofs, and intricate latticework, you can scarcely believe the building started life as a hôtel particulier before being transformed by antiques dealer Ching Tsai Loo in the 1920s. It's undoubtedly one of the most unusual architectural highlights in Paris. The only downside is that it's rarely open outside of private exhibitions, so you'll need to get lucky to look inside.

Musée Yves Saint Laurent

5 avenue Marceau, 16th
Closed Monday
museeyslparis.com

If fashion is your religion, this homage to France's most famous couturier is as close as you'll get to a place of pilgrimage. A compact yet reverential museum, it's situated in the designer's old atelier and opened to great acclaim in 2017. Thematic exhibitions touch on different periods in his life, from sketches made shortly after he moved to Paris from Algeria when he was aged just 18, to displays of collections defined by "imaginary travels" in India, China, and Japan. Depending on what's being shown when you visit, you might spot the peacoat worn in his first show or his once-radical tuxedo jacket that helped transform the world of womenswear. Other exhibits, such as his studio space, give a little more insight

CLOCKWISE FROM TOP LEFT: PARK MONCEAU; PAGODA PARIS; MUSÉE YVES SAINT LAURENT

into the personal life of the Petit Prince de la Mode, but contentious topics like drugs and sexuality are carefully avoided.

Palais de Tokyo

3 avenue du Président Wilson, 16th
Closed Tuesday
palaisdetokyo.com

Nowhere courts controversy like the Palais de Tokyo. Uncompromising in its approach, it stages cutting edge shows that constantly keep visitors on their toes, oscillating from light installations and multimedia works to performance pieces by the likes of Abraham Poincheval, who once lived inside a glass box here for a month, hatching eggs with his body heat while being peered at by curious gallery-goers. Information is minimal if present, and the sprawling multifloor gallery is all exposed concrete pillars and bare walls. Come prepared to fully immerse yourself in the experience. Outside, there's a concrete basin popular with skateboarders that offers great vistas across to the Eiffel Tower.

Musée d'Art Moderne de la Ville de Paris

11 avenue du Président Wilson, 16th
Closed Monday
mam.paris.fr

Despite its fantastic selection, the Musée d'Art Moderne de la Ville de Paris can come across as the Palais de Tokyo's depressingly straight-laced sibling. Absent are challenging installations and stark gallery spaces, and instead you'll find bright, well laid out collections, including paintings by Braque, Picasso, and Matisse and superb photography by the likes of Henri Cartier-Bresson. There's plenty to discover from artists you may never have heard of before, too, and as the galleries are smaller than at the Pompidou they're far more manageable to explore. In a rarity for Paris, the museum's permanent collection is also free to visit—so there's really no reason not to stop, even if your main destination is next door.

Crazy Horse

12 avenue George V, 8th
Two or three nightly shows, depending on the day and season
lecrazyhorseparis.com

If you want to see burlesque in Paris, forget about the traditional red light district around Pigalle and tumble down a risqué rabbit hole for a night of very nude cabaret at the Crazy Horse. Since opening in 1951, Le Crazy has remained the city's trendsetter, mixing the art of the striptease with high fashion. Their shows aim to celebrate beauty and femininity, with a mixed and often star-studded audience (past guests have included Cara Delevingne, Rihanna, and John Legend as well as fashion greats such as Jean Paul Gaultier). Even descending into the low-lit underground theater and settling into your red velvet seat, a glass of champagne in hand, is an experience in itself—but the staging, lighting, and immaculate choreography make this the best in the business. Beyoncé even used the cabaret as inspiration for her video, "Partition." Just don't overdo the champagne and go crazy yourself when buying merch on the way out—unless you're sure that whip will make it home in your suitcase.

Musée Guimet

6 place d'Iéna, 16th
Closed Tuesday
guimet.fr

An unexpectedly modern museum with three airy floors dedicated to the history of art in Asia, the Musée Guimet is one of the more unusual landmarks on the Paris museum scene—and really the only museum of its kind in Europe. It's not the most obvious place to seek out on a short visit to Paris, but it does present a rare chance to see ancient sculptures from Cambodia and Myanmar alongside beautifully woven clothing from Turkmenistan and blue-and-white porcelain from Japan. The exhibits get smaller and more interesting the higher you climb, transitioning from magnificent temple bronzes to opium pipes and snuff bottles, including some exhibits entirely amassed by private collectors, hidden during World War II and then donated to the state.

Cité de l'Architecture et du Patrimoine

1 place du Trocadéro et du 11 Novembre, 16th
Closed Tuesday
citedelarchitecture.fr

Mainly of interest to those who geek out on all things architecture and urban planning, this museum is missed by many as they clamor for the perfectly framed shot of the Eiffel Tower across the river. It covers France's built heritage from the Middle Ages to today, touching on themes as diverse as sustainable development to the evolution of painted décor and stained glass. The jewels in the museum's crown are the plaster casts and full-size reproduction murals that bring to life architectural highlights from across the country. Easier to frame in the context of Paris today are exhibits on contemporary architecture and the work of visionaries like Gustave Eiffel and Jean Nouvel, whose legacy is very much in evidence across the city.

Fondation Louis Vuitton

8 avenue du Mahatma Gandhi, 16th
Closed Tuesday
fondationlouisvuitton.fr

Incongruously sited in the sprawling woods of the Bois de Boulogne, the arresting Frank Gehry–designed Fondation Louis Vuitton is a relative newcomer to the city's contemporary art scene. Its architectural poetry will resonate with those familiar with Gehry's other buildings—among them the Walt Disney Concert Hall in Los Angeles and the Guggenheim Museum in Bilbao. Its soaring sail-like glass canopies are at once futuristic and classically beautiful, hiding a magnificent roof terrace as well as 11 exhibition galleries. There's no permanent collection here, but instead a roster of well-curated exhibitions that tend to run for six months or so at a time. They might include collaborations with MoMA or one-off curations of contemporary African art. Don't be put off by the schlep to get here and the lack of nearby attractions: It's well worth the journey.

COFFEE

Anticafé Louvre

10 rue de Richelieu, 1st
Open daily
anticafe.eu

Since the first Anticafé opened in 2013, a handful have sprung up across the city. This remains one of the best, with a mix of shared tables, comfy chairs, and window seats. The concept is simple: You pay by the hour (usually around €5) and included are unlimited barista-made coffees, soft drinks, snacks, and wi-fi.They call themselves a hybrid between a café and a coworking space, and particularly in the first arrondissement, they fill a much-needed gap in the market. Whether you need to interrupt your vacation to catch up on e-mails or simply need a space to while away a few hours and recharge without feeling guilty about only buying one drink, this is the perfect spot.

Café Kitsuné

51 Galerie de Montpensier, Jardin du Palais Royal, 1st
Open daily

In contrast to the stately marble arcades of the Palais Royal, this teeny café from Maison Kitsuné is as cool as they come. You'd even be forgiven for missing it, as it retains its original façade. The advert above the window for *filatures & tissages* (spinning and weaving) may be a throwback to a different era, but the menu is all about the latest trends. Coffees are supplemented by matcha hot chocolate and dirty chai; plus creations that range from iced coffee to iced yuzu are offered in the summer months. Their beans come from London's excellent Workshop Coffee roastery. Space inside is tight, so try to get one of their perfectly positioned tables outside in the gardens, usually somewhat pretentiously roped off.

PÂTISSERIE

Aki Boulanger

16 rue Sainte-Anne, 1st
Closed Sunday

Japanese flavors paired with classic French pâtisserie techniques is the culinary combination you've likely long been missing out on. We're talking matcha choux buns, yuzu éclairs, and authentic Japanese-style melon pan—all served in a casual corner bakery alongside traditional jambon-beurre baguettes and savory bento boxes. It's the sweet treats that really draw in the crowds though, especially seasonal specials like their take on a Mont Blanc, a mound of meringue, chestnut purée, and whipped cream. The setting is functional rather than atmospheric, so take your order to go and head for the grounds of the Palais Royal or the Tuileries.

La Pâtisserie des Rêves

19 rue Poncelet, 17th
Closed Monday

For a sugar fix near the Arc de Triomphe, head to La Pâtisserie des Rêves. This dreamy spot (its name literally means the "pâtisserie of dreams") on a busy market street in the 17th arrondisement is one of two shops in Paris founded by Philippe Conticini and Thierry Teyssier, and now run by Daniel Mercier. The cakes, tarts, and macarons here are designed to evoke childlike glee and wonder. Beneath distinctive glass cloches you might find classics like a saint-honoré or opéra, or beautiful creations such as a pistachio-raspberry Paris–Brest for around €8. Then there are *guimauves* (marshmallows), truffles, and madeleines. Look out for their *brioche feuilletée aux pralines roses*, too: this Lyonnaise specialty is studded with shards of uber-sweet pink pralines.

La Pâtisserie du Meurice par Cédric Grolet

6 rue de Castiglione, 1st

Closed Monday

Young chef Cédric Grolet took the world by storm with his imaginative, bold creations: life-like fruits sculpted on top of classical tarts and elaborate Rubik's Cubes constructed from 27 individual cakes. Although at first they were just served in the swag surrounds of hotel Le Meurice's restaurant, Le Dalì, word quickly got out, and in 2018 this bijou boutique opened to great furor as he was named the top pastry chef in the world. Now you can get a little taste of pâtisserie perfection to take away. For around €8–10 you can pick up an astonishingly beautiful tart; more elaborate pâtisseries (including the Rubik's Cube) cost up to €170. The displays are radically minimalist: There's just one example of each of the day's creations on an otherwise bare counter.

RESTAURANTS

Balagan

9 rue d'Alger, 1st

Open daily

balagan-paris.com

Meaning "beautiful mess" in Hebrew, Balagan is a collaboration between hoteliers and cocktail pioneers the Experimental Group and Israeli chefs Assaf Granit and Uri Navon. Their menu is a delight. You could make a meal of just the starters: figs with basil oil and lemon yogurt; kubaneh with tahini; freshly made fattoush salad. But the mains, around €30 and drawing inspiration from across the Middle East, are worth sticking around for, whether you're tempted by Persian-style sea bass or vegetarian options such as grilled eggplant. Of course, thanks to the cofounders, cocktails make an appearance, too. Their take on a Bloody Mary, with mezcal, vermouth, and beet syrup is just the thing to soothe a sore head.

Bistrot Victoires

6 rue de la Vrillière, 1st
Open daily

Old-timey but just far enough off the beaten track not to get mobbed, this lovely little bistro does budget-friendly classics with style. That means garlicky escargot for less than €10, steaks or duck confit for less than €15, and mountains of profiteroles for dessert. If you've not quite got room for that much chocolate and cream to finish, order a *café gourmand* (coffee with a miniature selection of desserts), a traditional option that you'll find on many French bistro menus. The atmosphere belies the low prices: spindle-backed chairs are set beneath arched gold mirrors and deco-style wall lights, and the service is refreshingly friendly.

Claus

14 rue Jean-Jacques Rousseau, 1st
Open daily
clausparis.com

There comes a point when you've had one too many rich breakfasts and inevitably crave a bowl of granola and a glass of freshly squeezed OJ. This white-on-white daytime-only café has you covered. The menu runs the gamut from pastries and porridge to omelets and potato rosti, but their specialty is the German treat *pfannkuchen* (a type of pancake). If you want to go big, for around €30 you can get a three-course breakfast including almost all of the above. Spot it by the geometric floor tiles and cloverleaf logo emblazoned on the exterior.

CLOCKWISE FROM TOP LEFT: LE MERMOZ; CONFIT DE CANARD AT BISTROT VICTOIRES; L'ECUME SAINT-HONORÉ; FRIED CHICKEN AT ELLSWORTH

L'Ecume Saint-Honoré

6 rue du Marché Saint-Honoré, 1st
Closed Sunday and Monday

Few sounds signal the start of a great lunch like the clang of discarded oyster shells hitting a metal pail. Add in a soundtrack of seagulls plus hand-painted seaside scenes on the wall, and you'll start to get a feel for this seafood bar. At the front it's still a proper fishmonger, but behind you can squeeze around high tables where staff will ply you with platters of just-shucked oysters and clams, and bottles of Pouilly-Fumé, until you admit defeat. Their lunchtime formule is a steal at less than €17 for six oysters, bread, butter, and a glass of wine, but you can rack up a much larger bill. Oysters are the main event, but everything from mussels and langoustines to marinated octopus and taramasalata miraculously appear from the midst of the shop.

Ellsworth

34 rue de Richelieu, 1st
Closed Sunday evening
ellsworthparis.com

A chic small-plates restaurant with a reputation for serving fried chicken is probably the last thing you'd expect to find steps from the Palais Royal. Yet Ellsworth is just that. Sister restaurant to the pricier wine bar Verjus around the corner, Ellsworth epitomizes the new wave of casual dining spots. Its decidedly cosmopolitan vibe is reflected not just on the menu—where you might find ricotta doughnuts and French toast for brunch before broccoli with bone marrow and chicken liver parfait at dinner—but by the expats who clamor to sit at its tables. Lines can form out the door, so check their opening hours online and get there 10 minutes before, or be sure to make a reservation. That said, the pick of the seats are those at the marble bar and are usually reserved for walk-ins.

Les Grands Verres

13 avenue du Président Wilson, 16th
Open daily
quixotic-projects.com

When Quixotic Projects—the collective behind staunch fashion-crowd favorites such as Candelaria and Glass—took over the vast restaurant at the Palais de Tokyo the result was only going to be superb. Their skill at creating one-of-a-kind concepts saw them soften the gallery's industrial aesthetic with a canopy of dangling light bulbs and sleek padded booths and bar seating. It's worth coming to eat here even if you're not stopping to see the art, although it would be a shame not to combine the two. Seasonality and sustainability underpin the menu (they even grow their own edible flowers) with inspiration drawn from the Mediterranean, Middle East, and beyond. You could find panzanella with a tahini dressing or buffalo mozzarella with kumquats before meatier main dishes (around €25) such as lamb with smashed kohlrabi or pork with smoked eggplant.

Le Mermoz

16 rue Jean Mermoz, 8th
Closed Saturday and Sunday

Just near the start of the Champs-Élysées is this unfussy bare-table bistro. A relative newcomer to the area but already holder of a Michelin Bib Gourmand, Le Mermoz offers superb value in a traditionally pricey part of Paris. The young team have stacked up some impressive experience at celebrated spots in Paris's foodier quartiers and are passionate about carefully sourcing ingredients, from the saucisson you can snack on when you arrive through to the slices of creamy Saint-Nectaire served before dessert (cheese always comes before sweets in France). Dishes are delicately plated and inventive: Black mullet might be paired with clementines, or cockles cooked in a light broth with peas and mint. In the evening, petites assiettes are served tapas-style from €10, while at lunch expect to pay up to €30 for larger plats.

Udon Bistro Kunitoraya

1 rue Villedo, 1st

Closed Wednesdays

kunitoraya.com

The streets just northwest of the Louvre, around rue Sainte-Anne, are sometimes known as Little Tokyo. Here you'll find some of the best udon, okonomiyaki, and yakitori in the city as well as a handful of restaurants specializing in Southeast Asian cuisine. If a steaming bowl of noodles is just what you need after hours of antiquities and architecture, Kunitoraya is the perfect choice. Their udon, served both in hot soups and cold, are the main attraction, although additional rice-based options include katsudon and chirashi-zushi. Seating is at shared tables with wooden stools—and you may have to wait to get in.

BARS

Bar Hemingway

15 place Vendôme, 1st

Daily from 6 p.m.

Without a doubt the most famous hotel bar in the city, the Ritz Hotel's Bar Hemingway might be outrageously expensive, but it's worth visiting both for its marvelous drinks and fascinating history. It's said that Hemingway liberated the bar from Nazi soldiers, after which he celebrated by buying everyone a bottle of champagne, or downing 51 martinis in a row, depending on who you choose to believe. War stories aside, it was inarguably a favorite haunt of the great writer, as well as F. Scott Fitzgerald and Gary Cooper. Today a beautifully made cocktail in the bar's elegant paneled salon will set you back around €30: Stick to the classics like a French 75 or a Manhattan.

Le Garde Robe

41 rue de l'Arbre Sec, 1st
Closed Sunday

Unpretentious and affordable wine bars are thin on the ground in this part of town, which makes Le Garde Robe a real find. You won't find any English menus in this pint-sized bar, but a great selection of natural and biodynamic wines are chalked up on the wall, along with a range of sharing planches and a dish or two of the day. Tell them what you like, and they'll happily suggest a wine you'd never thought of trying, perhaps an unusual Syrah and grenache blend from a small producer in the Rhône or something punchy from the Languedoc. It's the kind of spot where you can settle in for the evening and order cheese and charcuterie to your heart's content.

Le Musset

169 rue Saint-Honoré, 1st
Open daily
lemusset.paris

All corner cafés are not made alike—especially this close to the Louvre. With its smart navy awnings and mid-century vibe, Le Musset fits right in on glitzy rue Saint-Honoré, but it's also laid back enough to be an easy spot to rest weary legs come apéro hour. They do simple food (burgers, salads, and steaks) and even better drinks. Cocktails start at just €8, including classy takes on old favorites like Long Island iced teas and piña coladas, and there are plenty of wines by the glass. They're open until 2 a.m. every night of the week, so you might just find yourself staying longer than you intended.

SHOPPING

Astier de Villatte

173 rue Saint-Honoré, 1st
Closed Sunday
astierdevillatte.com

Enter dinner-party dreamland. You might not believe that this charming, almost ramshackle boutique was founded by friends Ivan Pericoli and Benoît Astier de Villatte in 1996. Its wooden shelves are seemingly haphazardly stacked with fine, crimped-edge porcelain that at first looks to be from a much older era. It's only when you pick up a dish or two that you realize this delicate tableware is a high-end modern take on classic French design, the perfect rustic-chic addition to a Hamptons cottage or villa in Provence. It's little wonder their plates, mugs, jugs, and candles have been picked up by luxury stores worldwide—and their original boutique now boasts the prices to match.

ASTIER DE VILLATTE

J'y Troque

7 rue Villedo, 1st
Closed Sunday

The idea that Parisians dress head-to-toe in Chanel and Dior simply isn't true—but if you want to pick up some high-end labels to take home, the city's *dépôts vente* (consignment stores) are the places to head. Some feel more like a sprawling rummage sale than a luxury shopping experience, but J'y Troque bucks the stereotype. It's one of the most pleasant and approachable places to browse, two neat rooms filled with racks of accessories and clothes by the likes of A.P.C., Isabel Marant, and YSL. On the more affordable end are cool tees and Hermès belts. With more cash to splash you could leave with a pair of Louboutin heels or a Louis Vuitton bag.

Maison Kitsuné

52 rue de Richelieu, 1st
Closed Sunday

Cofounded in 2002 by an ex-manager of Daft Punk, fashion brand and music label Kitsuné is a French tour de force. Once suitably caffeinated at their Palais Royal coffee shop, stop by their rue de Richelieu store around the corner to shop their ready-to-wear collection. It's split into men's and women's sections, but many designs happily span both. Bold slogan tees (a Parisian essential) start around €70, while you can expect to spend more than €100 for a pair of sneakers, high tops, or a sweatshirt. If bragging rights back home are top of your list, check out the baseball caps emblazoned with their trademark fox logo.

CHAPTER 2

Along the Seine

The banks of the Seine are where you'll find movie-romance Paris at its finest. Parisians really do line the banks with bottles of rosé and beers come sunset, weekend lunchtimes see fierce competition for the best picnic spots, and runners, roller-skaters, and cyclists exercise against the backdrop of some of the city's most famous sights. No trip is complete without at least a few hours strolling by the water, and if you're going to embrace Parisian clichés, this is the place to do it. Don your best Breton stripes for a game of pétanque by the riverside, cool down with a sorbet in summer, or sip hot chocolate to warm up on a windy winter morning walk.

Although the Seine is France's third-longest river, running all the way to the Normandy coast, it's inexorably tied to Paris. Not only does it divide the city culturally and geographically into the Left and Right Banks, it also played a significant role in the city's development from a small Roman outpost to a prospering medieval port, and eventually to the flourishing capital you see today. Nowhere else can you see the evolution of Paris so clearly. The stretch of river running from the Louvre to the Eiffel Tower has even been given UNESCO World Heritage status to mark its architectural and historical significance.

Recently, thanks to a forward-thinking initiative spearheaded by Mayor Anne Hidalgo, the river has also become much more pleasant to wander. Plans are underway to halve the number of cars in the city, and the pedestrianization of the riverside has been the first step. Once traffic-choked waterside rat runs have now been transformed into pleasant walkways protected as part of the Parc Rives de Seine, more than 4 miles of riverbanks interspersed with sidewalk games and cafés. Above them at street level are the 200 or so *bouquinistes* (stalls that have existed in some form since the 17th century). Today they mostly sell second-hand novels, art prints, and memorabilia, but the romantically inclined should picture Hemingway, Fitzgerald, and Orwell leafing through the paperbacks; they all reportedly browsed here.

Île de la Cité is the most natural place to start exploring. This is where Paris was founded as a small Celtic settlement, Parisii, in the

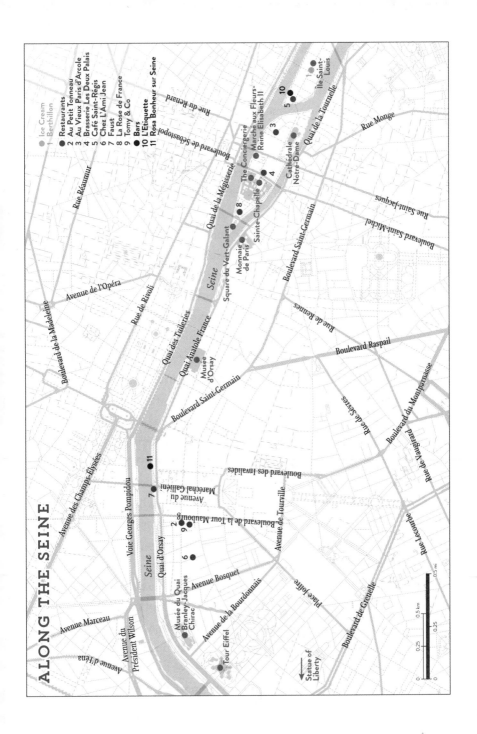

ALONG THE SEINE

Ice Cream
1 Berthillon

Restaurants
2 Au Petit Tonneau
3 Au Vieux Paris d'Arcole
4 Brasserie Les Deux Palais
5 Café Saint-Régis
6 Chez L'Ami Jean
7 Faust
8 La Rose de France
9 Tomy & Co

Bars
10 L'Etiquette
11 Rosa Bonheur sur Seine

third century BC and remains the city's heart. Here you'll find the loveliest river views, particularly from Square du Vert-Galant on the island's western point, as well as fire-scarred Notre-Dame Cathedral, the Conciergerie, and simply the mesmerizing chapel of Sainte-Chapelle, illuminated by a breathtaking series of stained-glass windows. Directly across the river on the Left Bank is the Monnaie de Paris. Part mint and part contemporary art gallery, it hosts some of the city's most interesting—if unexpected—exhibitions. By contrast there's little in the way of sights on neighboring Île Saint-Louis. This tiny and peaceful island draws you in with charming bistros, perfect for lazy long lunches.

It's a short walk from the islands to the Musée d'Orsay, once a train station and now the city's finest gallery celebrating the work of the Impressionists, including numerous works by Monet, Renoir, and van Gogh. If you visit one big museum on your trip, make it this one. Down at river level, the Berges de Seine celebrates a different sort of artistry. This was one of the first parts of the riverside to be redeveloped, and amid the floating gardens and workout areas you'll often spot murals, such as a magnificent rainbow flag painted for the city's Pride celebrations.

Following the course of the river farther eastward, keen-eyed travelers pause at Pont de l'Alma. Although no less than 37 bridges crisscross the river, the earliest dating back to the 1500s, Pont de l'Alma has special significance. The Zouave statue tucked under its arches is the city's unofficial flood measure; the waters usually lap several feet beneath the plinth but have risen above the statue's knees. The other reason to stop here is to visit the controversial Musée du Quai Branly, which explores world heritage and non-European cultures.

The obvious spot to conclude a day wandering the Seine is the Eiffel Tower, the city's instantly recognizable icon. Is it worth the climb? Not really. Unless you're ascending for a meal at the swanky restaurant Le Jules Verne, it's more enjoyable to take in the skyline from the deck of a floating bar, such as Rosa Bonheur sur Seine. Yet there is reason to venture beyond the Eiffel Tower. Perhaps the most curious sight in all of

Paris is the Statue of Liberty standing proudly by Pont de Grenelle; it's a quarter-scale exact replica of the New York original gifted to France by the United States in 1889.

BOAT TRIPS ALONG THE SEINE

One of the best ways to take in the sights along the river is to get out on the water. Sightseeing boats zip up and down the Seine day and night, but dusk is the most atmospheric time to take a trip. Time your journey right and you'll see the Eiffel Tower sparkling during its hourly illuminations as well as the Conciergerie and the Musée d'Orsay bathed in golden early-evening light.

There are a huge number of operators to choose from. Bateaux Mouches, Bateaux Parisiens, and the Vedettes du Pont Neuf are among the city's most famous cruises, and pack hundreds of passengers onto the deck of each boat in orange bucket chairs. At the other end of the spectrum are luxury private tours in sleek launches: Check out River Limousine and My Paris River as well as one-off Airbnb experiences. Dinner cruises usually aren't worth the expense; you're more likely to enjoy an hour or so expedition on the river, and then a meal somewhere special back on dry land.

CLOCKWISE FROM TOP LEFT: PONT ALEXANDRE III; THE EIFFEL TOWER; PASSERELLE LÉOPOLD SÉDARD SENGHOR

Île Saint-Louis

Stepping onto Île Saint-Louis, the smaller of the two islands, can feel like stepping back in time. The sleepy sister to Île de la Cité, it holds no sights as such, just one main road and a handful of peaceful side streets that split off toward the river. Some of the 17th-century mansions here remain as homes, others have become hotels, and a slew of cute if mostly touristy boutiques and cafés take up the street-level spots, mainly along the central rue Saint-Louis en l'Île. Be sure to stop at Paris's most famous ice-cream shop, Berthillon, before crossing onto Île de la Cité via Pont Saint-Louis, where buskers often set up on sunny days to provide (surprisingly good) free concerts.

Cathédrale Notre-Dame

6 Parvis Notre-Dame, 4th
notredamedeparis.fr

No other sight symbolizes the city like Our Lady of Paris, the Cathédrale Notre-Dame, first built in the Middle Ages and finally completed in the 15th century. When its roof dramatically caught fire during renovations in spring 2019, the city came to a standstill. Hymns were sung in the streets and millions of euros in donations poured in from around the world within hours. While many of the cathedral's treasured were saved, and thankfully no lives were lost, it remains to be seen how much restoration will be feasible—and how long it will take. Before the fire, somewhere in the region of 14 million visitors came to marvel at this Gothic masterpiece each year. At the time of writing, propositions were being considered for a temporary structure where worshipers could pay their respects, and it was still possible to admire its magnificent facade and flying buttresses.

Sainte-Chapelle

8 boulevard du Palais, 1st
Open daily
sainte-chapelle.fr

While it's hidden from view within the Palais de Justice, Sainte-Chapelle might just be Paris's worst kept secret. No matter your religious beliefs, this two-story gothic chapel is simply astounding. It was built in the 13th century by Louis IX to house Christ's crown of thorns and other holy relics.

THE UPPER CHAPEL AT SAINTE-CHAPELLE

Today, thanks to a recent round of restoration, it's just as mesmerizing to visit as it must have been when first built. It might not look much from the outside—and you wouldn't be the first to wonder if you've come to the right place—but the moment you walk into the lower chapel, it's clear this is somewhere really special. In this dark, low-ceilinged nave are glimpses of the church as it would have looked in the 1200s, the stone walls daubed in jewel-like sapphire tones and decorated with gold fleurs-de-lys. Yet the chapel's majesty is still to come. Scramble up the narrow staircase and you emerge, blinking into the light-flooded upper chapel. Here 15 stained-glass windows, each nearly 50 feet high, depict scenes from the Old and New Testament. Unlike the city's other churches, you have to pay to visit, but it's well worth the entrance fee.

The Conciergerie

2 boulevard du Palais, 1st
Open daily
paris-conciergerie.fr

You can't miss the Conciergerie as you stroll along the river. Its conical gothic turrets define Île de la Cité's skyline and are visible from all along the Right Bank. Although many delight in its sunset illuminations, far fewer take the time to delve into the building's fascinating history. It's one of the few vestiges of what was a royal palace, first established here in the 6th century, then abandoned in the late 14th century and later converted into a prison during the French Revolution. Its most famous resident was the last queen of France, Marie-Antoinette, whose cell you can visit today.

Marché aux Fleurs Reine Elizabeth II

Place Louis Lépine, 4th

In the midst of Île de la Cité's grand sites, little glimpses of local life remain. One of the most interesting is the Marché aux Fleurs, a permanent flower market that's been held here since 1830. The nod to the English monarch in the market's name was added in 2014 after Queen Elizabeth visited France to mark the 70th anniversary of D-Day. It centers on a series of open-sided greenhouses, packed with orchids, ferns, and pot plants. Traders have cottoned on to the fact that many of the casual browsers can't fit hydrangeas into their luggage, so you'll also find plenty more easily transportable souvenirs: lavender drawer sachets, scented soaps, and the like.

Square du Vert-Galant

15 place du Pont Neuf, 1st

The western end of Île de la Cité tapers into a sharp point, the ground dropping away behind Pont Neuf to a small park just a few meters above the Seine's usual water level. It's easy to miss if you don't go looking for

ÎLE DE LA CITÉ

it. This is one of the best spots to picnic while watching boats plying the Seine, perhaps staying to dangle your legs off the riverside pathway as the sun creeps toward the horizon. The only mystery? Why this indisputably triangular park has been dubbed a square.

Monnaie de Paris

11 quai de Conti, 6th
Closed Monday
monnaiedeparis.fr

The Monnaie de Paris, the Paris mint, might sound like the most prosaic of attractions, but thanks to its recent multimillion Euro "MétaLmorphose" transformation, it's well worth adding to your itinerary. In true Parisian style, it's somewhat perplexingly split: one part is the 11 Conti Museum and the other part consists of temporary exhibition spaces dedicated to contemporary art. The former takes a multisensory look at the mint's history and the craft of coin making. The latter sees 11 palatial rooms taken over by changing contemporary art shows for several months at a time. How the curation evolves is yet to be seen, but the first shows staged here have set a strong message about the future tone. First was Women House, which brought together the work of 40 female artists (including Martha Rosler, Cindy Sherman, and Laurie Simmons, mother to Lena Dunham) to examine women's confinement and their role in domestic spaces. Next up was France's first major show dedicated to British artist Grayson Perry whose ceramics, bronzes, and tapestries tackle subjects ranging from gender and sexuality to class and religion.

Musée d'Orsay

1 rue de la Légion d'Honneur, 7th
Closed Monday
musee-orsay.fr

Of Paris's big museums, the Musée d'Orsay is perhaps the most loved—and the most worth dedicating at least half a day to visiting. Built as the

Gare d'Orsay, a railway station for the Exposition Universelle of 1900, it's now the world's leading temple to Impressionism, housing works by the likes of Cézanne, Degas, Manet, Monet, Pissarro, Renoir, and van Gogh. Unlike in the Louvre, where you can barely see masterworks such as the Mona Lisa through the crowds, at the Musée d'Orsay you can usually find some space to actually appreciate the abundance of masterpieces on display. The only challenge is deciding where to start. If you've already fallen under Paris's spell, Renoir's *Bal du Moulin de la Galette*, depicting dancers in Montmartre, is perhaps among the most romantic of the gallery's paintings. Van Gogh's self-portrait, Cézanne's *The Card Players*, and Degas's *The Ballet Class* are among the works you may recognize from afar. More arresting is Courbet's *L'Origine du Monde*, a nude woman with her legs spread. This work is just as contentious today as it was when it was painted 1866, and it was recently the subject of a court case after Facebook banned users from posting the artwork to the site.

Musée du Quai Branly-Jacques Chirac

37 quai Branly, 7th
Closed Monday
quaibranly.fr

The modern Musée du Quai Branly, or Musée du Quai Branly-Jacques Chirac to give it its full but little-used name, has not been without controversy since it opened in 2006. Its permanent and temporary exhibitions cover "non-European cultures"—spanning wooden carvings from the Democratic Republic of Congo to headdresses from Vanuatu—with the aim of educating visitors about world heritage and culture. For some, the museum succeeds in its mission admirably, with the 350,000 or so items in its collections fostering greater cultural understanding and making up one of the most superb museums in the city. For others, including a *New York Times* writer who partially damned it as an attempt at "post-colonial recompense," its ethnographic approach still raises questions. Discussions around the repatriation of many of the museums artifacts are ongoing.

Tour Eiffel (Eiffel Tower)

Champ de Mars, 7th
Open daily from around 9:30 a.m. to midnight, with seasonal fluctuations
toureiffel.paris

The city's most famous symbol, the Tour Eiffel was only ever intended to be a temporary construction for the Exposition Universelle. Built in just two years, two months, and five days by Gustave Eiffel, with the help of engineers Maurice Koechlin and Émile Nouguier, plus architect Stephen Sauvestre, it attracted controversy right from the start. Yet somehow this 1,063-foot-high iron landmark has endured, becoming the most recognizable sight on the Parisian skyline. Locals might admire its hourly illuminations at night—it glitters from top to toe on the hour every hour for five minutes—but few would dream of actually climbing the tower itself. Prices depend on how high you go and how you get there. The cheapest tickets let you climb to the lowest level by stairs; the most expensive allow you to ascend to the top level in a glass-walled elevator. You can also come to eat at Le Jules Verne, the rather magical restaurant on the second level, of course with its own private entrance.

Statue of Liberty

Île aux Cygnes, 15th

A quarter-scale replica of the Statue of Liberty is probably the last thing you'd expect to spot in Paris, but Lady Liberty stands proudly on Île aux Cygnes, surveying the Seine as it streams past on either side of the city's third-largest island. The replica statue was gifted to France by the United States in 1889, just three years after the original was installed in New York, itself a gift from the French as a universal symbol of freedom and democracy. Today it stands as a mark of the bond between the two countries, fondly regarded by locals and visitors alike despite its improbable position. The best way to appreciate this most unlikely of attractions is from the river, although you'll need to make sure that your boat cruise will take you this far downriver.

ICE CREAM

Berthillon

29–31 rue Saint-Louis en l'Île, 4th
Closed Monday and Tuesday
berthillon.fr

The line usually running out the door and down the street is testament to the reputation of Berthillon's ice creams and sorbets. Unless it's really midwinter, you can't come to Île Saint-Louis without trying a *coupe* (scoop) or three of their superb creations. Classic French flavors should be the order of the day: perhaps an intense cassis sorbet if you're after something refreshing or a mix of *caramel au beurre salé* (salted butter caramel) and *chocolat noir* (dark chocolate) ice cream when you need a more indulgent option. Can't face the long line? Many of the other cafés on the road sell Berthillon's flavors. Just look out for the signs to make sure you're getting the real deal.

RESTAURANTS

Au Petit Tonneau

20 rue Surcouf, 7th
Open daily, Monday lunch only

One block back from the river between Les Invalides and the Musée du Quai Branly, things take a traditional turn at Au Petit Tonneau. After 80 years, they're still going strong with red-and-white Vichy tablecloths. Their nostalgic dishes regularly crop up on lists of food industry folks' favorite orders in the city: garlic-butter-drenched *escargots* (snails) to start, for less than €20; their famous *blanquette de veau* (veal stew); and a magnificent *carré d'agneau* (roasted rack of lamb) for around €30. For dessert, save room for a superb tart-meets-sweet lemon meringue pie.

Au Vieux Paris d'Arcole

24 rue Chanoinesse, 4th

Open daily

restaurantauvieuxparis.fr

Other than the façade of Notre-Dame itself, this pretty vine-draped restaurant might just be one of the most photographed spots on Île de la Cité, despite being hidden down a backstreet. They serve resolutely French dishes inspired by produce from the Aveyron region: *oeufs cocotte* (baked eggs) with foie gras, *sole meunière* (breaded and fried sole with a parsley-butter sauce), and *lapin moutarde* (rabbit with mustard). You can finish your meal with prunes in Armagnac or a vanilla-flecked crème brûlée. Expect to pay around €40 for three courses.

Brasserie Les Deux Palais

3 boulevard du Palais, 4th

Open daily

It may be in prime tourist territory opposite Sainte-Chapelle, but Brasserie Les Deux Palais still manages to turn on the charm. It offers everything you could desire in a Parisian brasserie, from green-stripe wicker chairs to gold-framed mirrors and art deco lighting. The cooking might not be haute cuisine, but they know their audience well. Expect to see lots of French onion soup, omelets, escargots, and homemade crêpes: the menu you expect to find at every bistro but often see diluted with foreigner-friendly additions. That said, it's a better spot for breakfast or lunch than an atmospheric dinner and generally closes up early.

Café Saint-Régis

6 rue Jean du Bellay, 4th

Open daily

cafesaintregisparis.com

The best spot for people watching on Île Saint-Louis, with views across to Île de la Cité, Café Saint-Régis is a retro delight: mirror-backed leather

CLOCKWISE FROM THE TOP: BERTHILLON; ROSA BONHEUR SUR SEINE; FAUST

banquettes, black-and-white tile floors, and big picture windows onto the street. Expect bistro staples on the menu from breakfast through to dinner: poached eggs, salmon burgers, steaks, tartare, and the like (mains around €20). Come cocktail hour, try a St-Germain spritz (made with the eponymous elderflower liqueur) or test your limits with a flaming glass of absinthe served from a traditional fountain at your table.

Chez L'Ami Jean

27 rue Malar, 7th
Closed Sunday and Monday
lamijean.fr

True gourmet addresses are in short supply near the Eiffel Tower, so it's little wonder this bistro is wildly popular. It's no simple steak-frites spot, but rustic fine dining with a Basque twist from chef Stéphane Jego. Settle in at a cozily spaced table for a not-so-light lunch or triumph of a tasting menu in the evening for around €80 (reserve ahead). You could find yourself tucking into everything from creamy sweetbreads with mushrooms or sea bream with figs, although pork often features heavily. For dessert, try their famous rice pudding—rather more special than it sounds.

Faust

Pont Alexandre III, 7th
Open daily
faustparis.fr

Somewhat of a chameleon, this bar-restaurant tucked under Pont Alexandre III transforms from a pleasant riverside terrace in the day to a rowdy, slightly pretentious club at night. Unless you're in the city to party, stop by at lunchtime to eat outdoors with the Seine lapping just meters from your feet and the Bateaux Mouches motoring by as they ferry sightseers up and down the river. The menu is simple—burgers, salads, and croques (toasted cheese sandwiches) mostly around €15—but it's the perfect spot to refuel as you wander along the riverbank.

La Rose de France

24 place Dauphine, 1st
Open daily
larosedefrance.com

While it may be the second royal square in Paris, Place Dauphine is much less visited than Place des Vosges just across the water. There's little in the way of sights to see but lots to admire, so settle in at en terrasse at La Rose de France, a family-run restaurant big on traditional cooking. For around €35 you can get two courses, perhaps a rich pumpkin velouté to start before a steak with bone marrow, their scallop "cassoulet," or a chicken breast stuffed with mushrooms on rosemary mash.

Tomy & Co

22 rue Surcouf, 7th
Closed Saturday and Sunday
tomygousset.com

Next door to Au Petit Tonneau, expect a rather different dining experience. Picking up a nod in the Michelin Guide in its first year of opening, this modern bistro is run by tattooed chef Tomy Gousset, previously of Daniel Boulud's restaurant Daniel in New York and more recently Pirouette in Paris. In the evening, a €70 tasting menu might take you through the likes of a fennel, orange, and endive salad with a velvet crab sauce, scallops on parsnip mash, and Brittany lobster with white beans, chorizo, and lemon confit. It's all exquisitely plated and perfectly balanced—a real special occasion spot. Lunch menus are a bit more affordable at around €30 for two courses.

BARS

L'Etiquette

10 rue Jean du Bellay-Ile Saint Louis, 4th

Closed Monday morning

letiquetteparis.com

Found the perfect sunny spot for a picnic by the Seine but don't know where to buy a great bottle of wine? Interested in a predinner wine workshop? This Île Saint-Louis wine shop and tasting room is your answer. Charming owner Hervé specializes in organic wines, many with no added sulfur, and not only is he passionate about championing small producers, but he delights in sharing his knowledge with newcomers. For formal tasting sessions it's best to get in touch to find out details, but shoppers can just show up.

Rosa Bonheur sur Seine

Quai d'Orsay, Port des Invalides, 7th

Open daily

rosabonheur.fr

Hop aboard this bar-boat for a drink on the Seine itself. Permanently moored by Pont Alexandre III, Rosa Bonheur sur Seine is a modern barge designed to evoke the spirit of a *guinguette* (one of the open-air cafés and dance halls that once lined the river), immortalized in Renoir's painting *Le Dejeuner des Canotiers*. But beyond the bar's inspiration, don't expect many similarities with the drinking culture of the 19th century. DJs replaced accordion players and snacks include French, Italian, and Spanish tapas, plus wood-fired pizzas. An on-deck apéro here after a visit to the Musée d'Orsay is sure to keep your night afloat.

CHAPTER 3

Around the Marais

Narrow medieval lanes, hidden courtyards, and charming cafés make the Marais one of the most enchanting quartiers in Paris. Spend a morning strolling the labyrinthine streets and you can't help but get lost in the area's storied past. Haussmann's grand boulevards are notably absent, and much of the architecture dates back to earlier periods.

It's hard to believe that a 13th-century fortress built by the Knights Templar once stood on the site of the Square du Temple's pretty gardens. It was later used to imprison royalty during the French Revolution—including Louis XVI on the eve of his execution—before being turned into a botanic garden in the late 1800s. Today the square marks the heart of the Haut Marais, the northern half of the quartier, one of the city's coolest neighborhoods. Here independent boutiques, jewelers, and stationery emporiums sit alongside hidden cocktail bars, great bakeries, and art galleries.

As you walk south, you enter more traditional territory. Here you'll find some of Paris's most fascinating small museums. The Musée de la Chasse et de la Nature, dedicated somewhat incongruously to both hunting and nature, is stuffed full of curiosities and elaborate taxidermy. Then there's the Musée Cognacq-Jay, a private collection of 18th-century art amassed in the early 1900s by Ernest Cognacq and his wife Marie-Louise Jaÿ. The spectacularly restored Musée Picasso needs no introduction. Farther south, things take a contemporary turn in the photography exhibitions at the Maison Européenne de la Photographie and at 59 Rivoli, the city's infamous art-squat.

To the west, you should also check out two resolutely modern landmarks in Beaubourg: the Forum des Halles and neighboring Jardin Nelson Mandela, the city's once gritty underground shopping center now transformed by a landmark redevelopment project, and the striking Centre Pompidou, home to the city's finest modern art collection.

The other big reason to come to the Marais is to do a spot of *lèche-vitrine,* as the French say (rather than going "window shopping" in France, you go "window licking"). Stores run the gamut from high

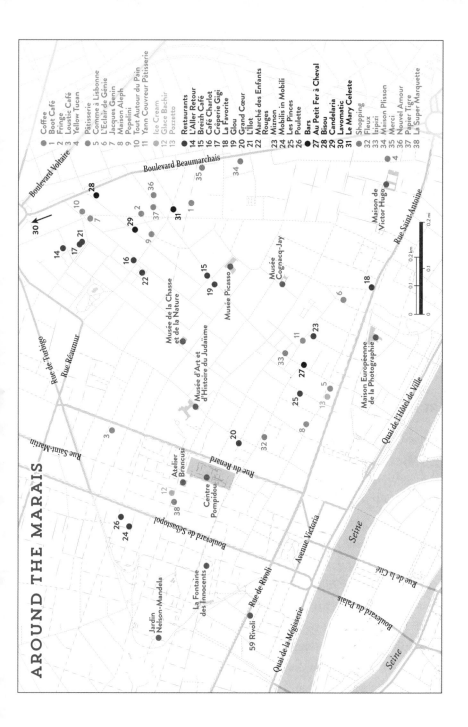

AROUND THE MARAIS

Coffee
1 Boot Café
2 Fringe
3 Loustic Café
4 Yellow Tucan

Pâtisserie
5 Comme à Lisbonne
6 L'Éclair de Génie
7 Jacques Genin
8 Maison Aleph
9 Popelini
10 Tout Autour du Pain
11 Yann Couvreur Pâtisserie

Ice Cream
12 Glace Bachir
13 Pozzetto

Restaurants
14 L'Aller Retour
15 Breizh Café
16 Café Charlot
17 Crêperie Gigi
18 La Favorite
19 Glou
20 Grand Cœur
21 L'Îlot
22 Marché des Enfants Rouges
23 Miznon
24 Mobilis in Mobili
25 Les Pinces
26 Poulette

Bars
27 Au Petit Fer à Cheval
28 Bisou
29 Candelaria
30 Lavomatic
31 Le Mary Celeste

Shopping
32 Fleux
33 Izipizi
34 Maison Plisson
35 Merci
36 Nouvel Amour
37 Papier Tigre
38 La Super Marquette

fashion to budget brands: think everything from Chanel and Cos to Aesop and Bonton.

Once you're shopped out, take a step back in time at the famous Place des Vosges, built by Henry IV. Surrounded by elegant arcades, today it's one of the rare places where you're allowed to laze on the grass on sunny days. Victor Hugo lived here from 1832 to 1848, residing in the Hôtel de Rohan-Guéménée, one of the 18th-century mansions that enclose the square, at the time he started work on *Les Misérables*. You can tour his apartment for free.

More recently the Marais was the heart of the city's Jewish quarter, a legacy that's evident in the wildly popular falafel shops that line rue des Rosiers and in the excellent Musée d'Art et d'Histoire du Judaïsme. Nearby is the sobering Mémorial de la Shoah, opened 60 years after the liberation of Auschwitz. Along the adjacent Allée des Justes are the names of nearly 4,000 people who risked their lives to help Jews in France during the Second World War.

SEE

Musée Picasso

5 rue de Thorigny, 3rd
Closed Monday
museepicassoparis.fr

Revamped and reopened five years ago, the Musée Picasso offers unrivaled insight into the artist's life. Amid the 5,000 artworks there are plenty of great masterpieces, including his celebrated Cubist paintings such as *Man with Guitar*. More interesting are Picasso's works you may be less familiar with: early sculptures, paper sketches, photographs, and the costumes and sets he designed for Sergei Diaghilev's Ballets Russes. The museum is set in the beautiful Hôtel Salé, once a private mansion, opened to house this collection in 1985; the works themselves were donated to the state by Picasso's heirs to avoid inheritance tax. It's a magnificent

CLOCKWISE FROM TOP LEFT: MAISON DE VICTOR HUGO; ARCHITECTURE IN THE MARAIS; MUSÉE PICASSO

MUSÉE PICASSO

setting—the central staircase is based on the one Michelangelo designed for the Laurentian Library in Florence—and was chosen to provide a contrast to the futurism of Centre Pompidou, built a few years previously.

Musée d'Art et d'Histoire du Judaïsme

71 rue du Temple, 3rd
Closed Monday
mahj.org

The Marais has been at the center of the Jewish community in Paris since the 13th century. Today's gentrification means that kosher restaurants and synagogues are squeezed in alongside chain stores and boutiques, but its history and that of the Jewish community in Paris haven't been forgotten. Learn more at the Musée d'Art et d'Histoire du Judaïsme, also known as mahJ, which looks at Jewish culture worldwide as well as in France. The permanent collection touches on both periods in history and religious traditions, including an interesting in-depth look at 20th-century Jewish art, with works by Marc Chagall, Ossip Zadkine, and Amedeo Modigliani, all of whom worked in Paris. Temporary exhibitions range from subjects as diverse as the legacy of Sigmund Freud to the photography of Lore Krüger.

Musée de la Chasse et de la Nature

62 rue des Archives, 3rd
Closed Monday
chassenature.org

Things get curiouser and curiouser at the unexpectedly elegant Museum of Hunting and Nature. It doesn't exactly glorify hunting, rather it offers a somewhat romanticized look at the relationship between man and beast through history. There are curio cabinets with drawers to peer into; collections of guns, horns, dog collars, and figurines; and exquisite tapestries and paintings, some part of collections held by the Louvre. Don't miss the unicorn room, a tiny chamber dedicated to this mythical creature. Other displays, such as an antique wooden horse caged alongside a modern plastic heart sculpture, defy explanation. The astonishing trophy room is the most affecting attraction, its walls lined with meticulous taxidermy including tigers, cheetah, puma, gazelles, and a brown bear frozen in time rearing up on its hind legs. An animatronic boar that grunts as you approach it slightly detracts from the atmosphere but keeps kids happy.

Maison de Victor Hugo

6 place des Vosges, 4th
maisonsvictorhugo.paris.fr
Closed Monday

It's free to visit the apartment where the fêted author, playwright, and poet Victor Hugo lived on Place des Vosges from 1832 to 1848, restored not as when he lived there, but to showcase collections from different parts of his life. One room exhibits family portraits, another is decorated in the style of the quarters he designed for his mistress when they were in exile in the Channel Islands. You can also see the modified standing desk where he wrote (an idea far ahead of its time), and step into the morbid yet faithful reconstruction of the room where he died across the city on avenue d'Eylau, later renamed avenue Victor Hugo in his honor. Sadly, there's little reference to this most famous works, *The Hunchback of Notre-Dame* and *Les Misérables*.

Musée Cognacq-Jay

8 rue Elzevir, 3rd
Closed Monday
museecognacqjay.paris.fr

Unlike many galleries in Paris, the Musée Cognacq-Jay isn't dedicated to the work of one artist—or even one artistic style. This Marais mansion-musée is filled with the personal acquisitions of Ernest Cognacq and his wife Marie-Louise Jaÿ, founders of the Samaritaine department store. On their death they bequeathed their extensive collection of 18th-century art to the city, and it's been open to the public in this location since the 1990s. It's an eclectic but exceptional mix from the Age of Enlightenment, including sculptures, furniture, and snuff boxes as well as paintings by Canaletto and Fragonard. It's well worth exploring if you prefer to admire art on a smaller scale—and it's one of the few museums in Paris that's free to visit.

Atelier Brancusi

Place Georges Pompidou, 4th
Closed Tuesday, open afternoons only

In another of Paris's few free museums, you can learn more about the life and work of Romanian-born sculptor Constantin Brâncuși, who lived in Paris until his death in the 1950s. This small gallery, a faithful recreation of his studio, which he bequeathed to the French state, houses hundreds of his sculptures and sketches. It's a special spot to visit: His studio wasn't just his working space but an artwork itself, each piece arranged to be in perfect harmony. This reconstruction sits in an easily missable low-rise building designed by Renzo Piano, just next to the Centre Pompidou, and is well worth visiting at the same time as the Musée National d'Art Moderne. If you want to see more of his work, look out for *The Kiss* that marks the grave of his friend Tania Rachevskaia in southern Paris.

Centre Pompidou

Place Georges-Pompidou, 4th
Closed Tuesday
centrepompidou.fr

Multicolored pipes snake around the outside of Richard Rogers and Renzo Piano's famous "inside-out" building. Inside, as well as a cinema and a library, is the Musée National d'Art Moderne. This contemporary art collection is simply unrivaled, with only 5 percent of the works on display at any one time. Skip paintings by the likes of Matisse and Warhol for installations by lesser-known French artists such as Jean Dubuffet, whose monochrome sculpture *Le Jardin d'Hiver* you can actually climb inside. The top floor hosts interesting exhibitions that might range from Walker Evans's depression-era photography to David Hockney's vivid paintings of Los Angeles. Refuel at the rooftop Brasserie Georges before you leave: It's pricey if you want a full meal, but it's the perfect place for a hot chocolate with a view.

La Fontaine des Innocents

Place Joachim-du-Bellay, 1st

The crowds that today mill about Place Joachim-du-Bellay near the Forum Des Halles belie the square's grizzly past. As late as the 18th century this site was used as a huge graveyard, the Cimetière des Innocents. After it became overwhelmed in the late 1700s—the press of bodies was so great it's said they started to protrude through the walls of nearby cellars—the remains interred here were unceremoniously dug up and intact skeletons were moved to Les Catacombes de Paris. The latter are now a macabre tourist attraction in the 14th arrondissement, and all that marks the cemetery itself is the Fontaine des Innocents, a Renaissance-style fountain at the square's center decorated with carvings of frolicking nymphs.

Jardin Nelson Mandela

Passage de la Canopée, 1st

There's little reason to visit the Forum des Halles itself, unless you're hankering for some chain-store shopping or trip to the multiplex cinema, but the adjacent Jardin Nelson Mandela is delightful. Decades ago the city's main indoor market stood here, and once it closed the area slipped into decline, becoming one of the most insalubrious spots in the midst of Paris, distinguished only as the home of the world's biggest subway station, Châtelet-Les Halles. A redevelopment project over the past few years has seen it transformed. A new roof, La Canopée, has literally shone new light into the atrium of the multilevel subterranean shopping mall, and the surrounding land has been reclaimed to form a much-needed green space. There's a play park for kids, bandstand, and plenty of spots just to sit and soak up the sun.

59 Rivoli

59 rue de Rivoli, 1st
Closed Monday
59rivoli.org

Only in Paris could an illegal squat become one of the city's coolest gallery spaces—and its messy, art-adorned exterior remains unchanged on a road now lined by H&M, Zara, and Sephora. First occupied by artists in 1999, before being closed down and subsequently reopened with government approval, it retains a strong countercultural vibe. The five floors of crowded work and gallery spaces are linked by a narrow graffiti-covered staircase and play host to 15 permanent artists and 15 rotating visitors.

59 RIVOLI

Some are more commercially minded than others, with card payment machines and luggage carry-on-sized canvases. On Saturdays and Sundays, stop by for the evening concerts on the ground floor.

Maison Européenne de la Photographie

5/7 rue de Fourcy, 4th
Closed Monday and Tuesday
mep-fr.org

In another of the Marais's beautiful 18th-century mansions, this superb photography gallery is second only to the Jeu de Paume in its exhibitions—although some would argue it should hold the top spot in the city. Reopened at the end of 2018 with a landmark exhibition by street artist JR, the MEP showcases cutting-edge work by little-known and well-known photographers in France and beyond, from Vincent Perez's portraits examining cultural identity to Daoud Aoulad Syad's shots of daily life in Morocco. There's also a huge photo and video library here, and regularly scheduled guided tours are available if you want to get beneath the surface of this often-underappreciated art form.

COFFEE

Boot Café

19 rue du Pont aux Choux, 3rd
Open daily

Whether or not this is really the city's smallest café remains up for debate, but it's certainly one of the sweetest, set in an old *cordonnerie* (cobbler shop) with just a handful of tables. Behind the façade's peeling blue paint you can expect chemex filter coffees, superb hot chocolates, and rich *café crèmes* (espresso topped with gently frothed milk, usually less airy than a cappuccino). If you can get a table, order a slab-sized brownie or a cookie, or take your coffee for a stroll in one of their distinctive boot-stamped to-go cups.

Fringe

106 rue de Turenne, 3rd
Closed Tuesday

The Marais is the perfect neighborhood for idle weekend wandering, ideally with a coffee in hand. If you're looking for a beautifully made cappuccino or iced latte to go, this unpretentious café is the spot to choose. Opened by photographer Jeff Hargrove, it has all the "cool coffee shop" credentials (single origin beans, soy milk, etc.) but lacks some of the attitude. The walls are used to showcase interesting photography, and unusual crumpled-paper lights hang above the tables. You won't find the ubiquitous banana bread here either. The menu focuses on Scandinavian-style dishes: granola in the morning, open sandwiches at lunch, and cinnamon buns mid-afternoon.

Loustic Café

40 rue Chapon, 3rd
Open daily

This endearing espresso bar is one of the city's specialty coffee stalwarts. In collaboration with Antwerp-based roastery Cafénation, they're scientific in their approach to single-origin coffee. Come for a killer espresso or cold brew and be sure to save room for something sweet: S'mores cakes and homemade snickers bars might be among their American-inspired treats. Seats are in short supply, so it's not somewhere to linger for long.

Yellow Tucan

20 rue des Tournelles, 4th
Open daily

This bright, light little coffee shop gets everything right. There are no toucans in sight, but lots of yellow accents, from the sunshine yellow stools to the vases of daisies on the tables. In summer, benches outside are the perfect spot to bask in the morning sunshine. They have a simple formula: espressos, cappuccinos, cafés allongés, and the like to drink in and takeaway, and a small selection of cakes, cookies, and madeleines to go with them. If you're after a little cross-channel fusion, try the scones served toasted with salted French butter and jam. Their USB charging points are also a savior if you've left your adaptor at home.

PÂTISSERIE

Comme à Lisbonne

37 rue du Roi de Sicile, 4th

Daytime only, closed Monday

Have you discovered the cult status of Portugal's most famous pastry, the pastel de nata? If not, don't leave the Marais without a quick stop at this hole-in-the-wall bakery. Their superb custard tarts rival any Lisbon original: flaky puff pastry surrounding a light and creamy cinnamon-flavored filling. Demand is so high that you can even reserve online in bulk and specify your pick-up time. The adjoining restaurant, Tasca, is run by the same team and sells a range of gourmet Portuguese specialties including tinned sardines and organic *flor de sal* (sea salt) from the Algarve to bottles of olive oil and vinho verde.

L'Éclair de Génie

14 rue Pavée, 4th

Open daily

leclairdegenie.com

When éclairs are this good, one bakery quickly spawns more across the city—and several overseas. Christophe Adam's éclairs might cost upward of €5 a pop, but no one seems to care. If you want a mid-afternoon pâtisserie pick-me-up, go for something citrusy and fresh like raspberry and passion fruit or lemon and yuzu. For sheer indulgence, you can't beat the French classic *caramel au beurre salé* (salted butter caramel) or their combination of Madagascan vanilla and candied pecans. Devouring them on the street is definitely encouraged, but you can also get them boxed up. Nothing says vacation decadence like eating éclairs in bed.

Jacques Genin

133 rue de Turenne, 3rd

Closed Monday

Jacques Genin is *the* Parisian chocolatier to visit and this airy boutique meets tearoom is a fitting temple to his craft. Not only does he supply many five-star hotels around the city, but his creations are renowned among chefs the world over. Start by exploring his classical chocolates, sumptuous squares flavored with the likes of rosemary, fresh mint, and honey. Then move on to the confiserie: He's famous for his intense mango-passion fruit caramels and vegetable pâtes de fruits—perhaps even featuring beetroot or red pepper, depending on the season. If you stay for tea, treat yourself to the pâtisseries: lime and basil tartlettes, vanilla millefeuilles, and an airy, barely sweet cheesecake. If you dare, ramp up the sugar with a cup of super thick and super sweet hot chocolate.

Maison Aleph

20 rue de la Verrerie, 4th

Open daily

Levantine flavors meet French pâtisserie techniques in this Marais bakery, run by Aleppo-raised Myriam Sabet. If you've got a sweet tooth, you can't help but fall for her 1001 feuilles, a delicate take on baklava, and her bite-sized angel hair nests flavored with everything from orange flower water and fresh strawberries to dark chocolate and sumac. Summer means freshly churned ice cream, perhaps with rosewater or sesame, halva, and apricot. There's not much space to eat in the shop, so most people stop to take a picture of the pretty blue-tiled floor and pick up a selection to take away. Only the most disciplined can resist opening the box for a quick taste before they're out the door.

TOP: ÉCLAIR DE GENIE; BOTTOM: MAISON ALEPH

Popelini

29 rue Debelleyme, 3rd
Closed Monday
popelini.com

Forget about stacks of soggy profiteroles drenched in chocolate sauce, in Paris cream puffs take a more refined turn. At bakery Popelini, macaron-sized choux buns are an art form, individually iced and laid out in rainbow rows. You build your own takeaway box of four, six, or twelve flavors, so you can mix and match as you please. They're all made by hand, with top-quality ingredients like Madagascan vanilla and Valrhona chocolate. Classics include coffee, pistachio, salted caramel, and lemon, and there are seasonal specials that could feature anything from blood orange to *marrons glacés* (candied chestnuts). This is the first branch, but it's been so successful there are now several more.

Tout Autour du Pain

134 rue de Turenne, 3rd
Closed Saturday and Sunday

No trip to Paris is complete without at least one jambon-beurre eaten on a park bench for lunch. And there are few better places to pick up one of these crusty ham-and-butter baguette sandwiches than Tout Autour du Pain. This traditional Haut Marais boulangerie has scooped numerous awards for their baguettes and croissants. In the morning stop by for a perfectly flaky pain au chocolat or sate your sweet tooth mid-afternoon with a *chausson aux pommes* (apple turnover).

Yann Couvreur Pâtisserie

23bis rue des Rosiers, 4th
Open daily

Few places show Parisians' passion for pâtissierie like the lines for Yann Couvreur's sleek store. Its location is a marked change from the baker's first pâtisserie in the 10th, drawing more visitors than locals, but his skill remains evident throughout. Minimalist display cases keep all the attention on his intricately decorated and perfectly baked *financiers* (oblong almond cakes, here flavored with vanilla and sea salt), sables, and madeleines. Highlights include the individual raspberry and tarragon tarts and the glitter-topped chocolate mousse—perfect for a pique-nique. There's also a take-away-only window for ice cream.

ICE CREAM

Glace Bachir

58 rue Rambuteau, 3rd
Daily from noon to around 11 p.m.

This is Beirut-based Glace Bachir's first outpost in Paris, and, oh boy, is it worth the lines. The family business was founded in the 1930s but only opened in the French capital in 2017, bringing their organic ice creams to new legions of fans, including Lebanese expats, visitors, and Parisians alike. Their range mixes the flavors of the Middle East (rose petals, almond, orange flower) with crowd-pleasing classics (strawberry, vanilla, chocolate). Best of all you can have your scoop topped with whipped cream, rolled in pistachio nuts, or blended into a creamy milkshake.

Pozzetto

39 rue du Roi de Sicile, 4th
Daily from around noon

If you see someone stopping to lick a melting ice-cream cone in the south of the Marais, they've more than likely stopped by Pozzetto. This café does big business on sunny days, and their gelato is city-renowned. It's made by the traditional Italian method, using less cream and fat, and they stick to only authentic flavors. For something refreshing, mix a scoop of strawberry sorbet with one of *fiordilatte* (gelato simply made with milk and cream) or indulge in a double scoop of rich and chocolatey *gianduja*, the grown-up answer to frozen Nutella.

RESTAURANTS

L'Aller Retour

5 rue Charles-François Dupuis, 3rd
Open daily
laller-retour.com

It can be hard to find good steak-frites in Paris without a line of expectant foreigners snaking out the door. But somehow this low-lit little restaurant just off Place de la République remains pleasingly off the radar. Perhaps it's because you won't find any steakhouse clichés here: no bow-tie-clad waiters, no vintage movie posters, and no terrasse. Instead the focus is on the meat. Around €20 will get you the cut of the day, fries, and a salad. Spend a little more for classics like a côte de bœuf to share, or a little less for tartare, burgers, and carpaccio. The options are severely limited for vegetarians, but oenophiles will be in heaven with an extensive and affordable wine list ranging from big and bold Bordeauxs to lovely, light Burgundies.

Breizh Café

109 rue Vieille du Temple, 3rd
Open daily
breizhcafe.com

For many people there's only one spot for authentic Breton galettes in Paris, and that's Breizh Café, a Marais fixture for more than 15 years. A line permanently snakes down the road to its door at the weekend, as fans from around the world (they also have several outposts in Japan) pack in for buckwheat galettes, cider, and crêpes. You can't go wrong with a *galette complète* (egg, cheese, and ham) or one topped with smoked salmon and crème fraîche to start, then a crêpe drenched with Brittany's famous salted butter caramel to finish. The origin of this delicious combination dates back to the 1500s, when the region was exempt from France's salt taxes and the salt-and-sweet sauce was born. You can pick up jars to take home at their épicerie next door.

Cafe Charlot

39 rue de Bretagne, 3rd
Open daily
cafecharlotparis.com

White subway-tiled walls and vintage mirrors make this chic Parisian café the perfect spot to refuel with a French classic like a *croque-madame* (a fried ham-and-cheese sandwich with an egg on top). On a sunny day, it's worth fighting the impossibly well-dressed locals for a table outside, where you can sip rosé and people watch for hours on end. The staff know the seats will always be in demand, so expect the service to match.

Crêperie Gigi

4 rue de la Corderie, 3rd
Closed Monday
gigi-restaurant.fr

Like many spots in the Haut Marais, Crêperie Gigi is a little less traditional than some of its southern counterparts. You can get all the savory classics here—including time-tested galette flavor combinations like ham and comté, or goat's cheese, onions, spinach, and honey—but also more exciting ideas, ranging from miso chicken to burratina with pesto and cherry tomatoes. For dessert, their crêpes are sweet, sweet, sweet, the toppings heavy on cream, chocolate, and ice cream. They also serve both crêpes and galettes in apéro-sized sharing portions, ideal if you've not yet adapted to the Parisian habit of sitting down to dinner sometime after 9 p.m.

La Favorite

4 rue de Rivoli, 4th
Open daily

The Marais's delightful narrow lanes leave it sorely lacking when it comes to one thing: the sunny sidewalk tables so loved by Parisians. Perhaps this goes some way to explain the popularity of La Favorite, a smart but simple corner café on rue de Rivoli. They squeeze an astonishing number of tables onto their little stretch of sidewalk, and keep them toasty with heaters in winter. It's got all the trappings you'd expect—bright red awnings, waiters in black braces and white aprons, hot chocolate so thick you almost need to eat it with a spoon—plus a little bit of attitude. Come for a coffee or a glass of wine and if you want to eat, stick to classics like croque-monsieurs and burgers.

Glou

101 rue Vieille du Temple, 3rd
Open daily

Clever but simple cooking coupled with a great wine list makes Glou a much-loved spot among gourmets in the Marais. It's modern but not trendy and serious but not stuffy. In summer the doors are thrown open to include a few precious tables on the street: a dreamy spot to sip a glass of champagne against the backdrop of the Musée Picasso. Inside it's much cozier, an exposed stone wall on one side and a mural on the other—and usually a great soundtrack. Dishes range from steak tartare and gnocchi to scallop ceviche and grilled octopus, with main courses around the €20 mark.

Grand Cœur

41 rue du Temple, 4th
Open daily

Blink and you'll miss the Grand Cœur's pretty courtyard, tucked down a side street off rue du Temple. Under its lamp-lit canopy are 20 or so tables neatly set with white cloths; there are more inside in the smart dining room beneath artfully distressed antique mirrors. As well as offering a rather romantic place to eat away from the Marais's crowds, this brasserie is also surprisingly good value. You can get a two-course lunch menu for less than €25—perhaps an asparagus tart or octopus with chickpeas and then a more classic lamb dish. Plats rise to €30 in the evenings.

CLOCKWISE FROM THE TOP: GNOCCHI AT GLOU; HOT CHOCOLATE AT LA FAVORITE; YELLOW TUCAN

L'Ilot

4 rue de la Corderie, 3rd
Closed Sunday and Monday
laller-retour.com

L'Ilot, sister restaurant to L'Aller Retour, turns its attention to a different French specialty: seafood. At its casual sidewalk benches and bar tables you can pluck *bulots* (sea snails) from their shells, slurp platter after platter of salty oysters, and get your fingers sticky cracking crab legs and dunking *crevettes grises* (small grey shrimp) into mayonnaise. For dessert there's the Breton specialty *kouign-amann* (a crispy, buttery pâtisserie marvel), or more refreshing but no less indulgent creations like lime-meringue tarts. To drink, white wines are the order of the day. Try a Loire Valley Muscadet or a Sauvignon, both classic matches with shellfish.

Marché des Enfants Rouges

39 rue de Bretagne, 3rd
Closed Monday

The oldest market in Paris is now one of the hippest places to hang out on the weekend. The narrow rows of stalls are no longer home to fruit and vegetable sellers; instead you'll find authentic Moroccan couscous, Lebanese flatbreads, Neapolitan-style pizza, and Chez Alain Miam Miam's famous crêpes. There's not a lot of seating space in the market itself, so stop at the outdoor tables of L'Estaminet des Enfants Rouges for a drink before ordering food and then eat in the nearby Square du Temple.

Miznon

22 rue des Ecouffes, 4th
Closed Saturday

Those in the know skip the falafel joints on rue des Rosiers and head to loud, busy, and buzzy Miznon instead. Their Israeli-style pitas are fresh and filling, overstuffed with herbs, salad, and your choice of meat or veg— the lamb meatballs are superb. On the side add charred cauliflower or artichokes, and don't forget to go big on the sauces. You might end up spending a bit more at Miznon than at nearby hole-in-the-wall options, and it can be chaotic at times, but it's well worth a little splurge. Indeed, Miznon's popularity has even spawned a second branch by the Canal Saint-Martin.

Mobilis in Mobili

94 rue Saint-Denis, 1st
Open daily
customseafood.fr

Concept restaurants often take things too far, but this large and airy seafood bar has a simple and winning formula. You can customize your platter however you want, choosing how you'd like each item cooked and served. You could kick off with crab bisque or a selection of raw clams to start, then move onto *moules* (mussels) in a spicy Thai sauce or a salt-crusted sea bass. Wine comes by the carafe, glass, or bottle; plus there are a couple of beers on tap. It's definitely no-frills and service can be a little chaotic, but the quality is decent—and who's complaining when you can build your own seafood feast for less than €30?

Les Pinces

29 rue du Bourg Tibourg, 4th
Open daily
lespinces.com

Do you like your décor and your menu options simple? At Les Pinces, you have just four options: a whole grilled lobster, a lobster roll, a steak, or a surf-and-turf combo. The lobsters are sourced from Brittany, Canada, or America depending on the season, and come with chips and salads for around €25. For dessert, there's cheesecake or chocolate mousse. Tables are bare but service is attentive. They've clearly got their claws into a winning formula, and have now rolled out their concept into three restaurants around the city.

Poulette

3 rue Étienne Marcel, 1st

Open daily

pouletterestaurant.com

The simply gorgeous interior at this bistro is reason enough to come. Nearly every inch is covered in beautiful Belle Époque tiling, framing antique mirrors, and depictions of Greek-style goddesses. It's a clever contrast against the scuffed wooden chairs and zinc bar. The food is pleasingly much less fancy, too: They focus on seasonal bistro classics accompanied by cocktails, wines, and fresh-pressed juices. The menu is short, sweet, and affordable: perhaps asparagus or soup to start, ratatouille or steak for the main, then a panna cotta for dessert.

BARS

Au Petit Fer à Cheval

30 rue Vieille du Temple, 4th

Open daily

It can be hard to pick a traditional café in the Marais; they all tempt you in with their smart awnings, shiny bars, and waistcoated wait staff. Yet this tiny spot, named for its horseshoe-shaped bar and distinguished by the art nouveau signs that decorate its royal-green frontage, has to be one of the most atmospheric. It was first opened in 1903, but has been subsequently finessed and restored. Come to perch at the bar with a pichet of their *vin du mois* (wine of the month) before dinner, stop to drink a smoky Assam tea on a sidewalk table in the afternoon, or end your night by swirling a classic digestif like calvados or Armagnac beneath the heaters.

Bisou

40 rue Chapon, 3rd

Open daily

Meaning "kiss," Bisou is a recent and uber-cute addition to the Marais' bar scene. This cocktail spot isn't just passionate about their pink-hued decor but also sustainability and seasonality. Plastic straws are firmly off the menu and only French ingredients go into their cocktails. Even leftover fruit peels are dehydrated and transformed into edible garnishes. There's no drinks list, so share your favorites and expect to be inspired.

Candelaria

52 rue de Saintonge, 3rd
Open daily
quixotic-projects.com

Slink past the handful of tables at what appears to be an innocuous taco joint and you'll find a romantic and candlelit cocktail bar hidden behind. Candelaria was recently named one of the world's top 20 cocktail bars, but it's young, fun, and decidedly laid-back. At about €10–15 a pop, drinks on the agave-heavy cocktail menu are incredibly good value, or you can splash out on a mezcal flight for €30.

Lavomatic

30 rue René Boulanger, 10th
Closed Sunday and Monday

This little laundromat just off Place de la République isn't what you'd expect. Rather than the scourge of life in tiny Parisian apartments without washing machines, this laverie is actually the entrance to a secret speakeasy. Not that you'd guess unless you know where you're going: even the machines seem real enough, the soap trays full of water, and the drums big enough to climb inside. But press the right button and the back wall will spring open to reveal a tiny staircase leading up to the bar. Here you can perch on a swing seat or on a Brillo Pad stool and enter cocktail wonderland. Although they also serve wine and beer, you'll be missing out if you don't try one of their original creations like Basil Instinct, a gin cocktail with lemon, elderflower, and cucumber.

Le Mary Celeste

1 rue Commines, 3rd
Open daily
quixotic-projects.com

Sister bar to Candelaria, Le Mary Celeste first made its reputation as a seafood and wine spot, but now the concept is a little more fluid. Staff have denim aprons rather than old-school uniforms, and the wonky brick floors and geometric stained glass windows make it super relaxed—even if you're drinking champagne and throwing back oysters. You can stop by for a beer and a snack at one of the wooden bar tables, or dive into the cocktail menu, which ranges from simple summery numbers like clementine-infused vodka tonics to tequila, aquavit, and grapefruit combos. Come early or settle in for dinner: snacking plates to share from the raw bar, interesting salads, and spins on classic dishes like braised lamb shoulder.

SHOPPING

Fleux

39 rue Sainte-Croix de la Bretonnerie, 4th
Open daily
fleux.com

If your home is missing a set of melamine mugs printed with French scenes, a neon banana nightlight or Scandi-style tableware (who's isn't?), check out this homewares emporium, which refreshingly doesn't take itself too seriously. It's a treasure chest of unusual gifts, split into three shops. Across the showroom-style stores, you'll find faux flower arrangements and quirky ornaments alongside small selections of sunglasses and fair-trade jewelry. They also sell larger furniture—although this is only worth perusing if you're planning to furnish a Parisian pied-à-terre.

Izipizi

46 rue Vieille du Temple, 4th
Open daily
izipizi.com

It's summer all year-round at Izipizi's sweet little flagship store. Their cheap yet chic range of unisex glasses and sunglasses (from €35) reflect the simplicity of French street style. Think a hint of Ray-Ban with added city-chic: bold round frames in black, tortoiseshell, and pastel hues. Some styles are foldable, perfect if you're prone to breaking your glasses and want a pair you can throw in a pocket. Prefer the slopes to the sand? Check out their Glacier ski range with ramped-up UV protection.

Maison Plisson

93 boulevard Beaumarchais, 3rd
Open daily
lamaisonplisson.com

The place to get a gourmet fix in the Marais, Maison Plisson is split into a restaurant and food hall—but it's the latter you should at least pop in to see. Its shelves are packed with things you're just *sure* you need to buy: coffee beans roasted by Paris-based Belleville Brûlerie, cookies from Brussels' famous Maison Dandoy, and wickedly addictive black truffle potato chips from Spanish brand Torres. It's the kind of place where your euros seem to practically jump out of your wallet. Becoming a superfan already? Pick up a souvenir tin mug or printed dishcloth instead.

MERCI

Merci

111 boulevard Beaumarchais, 3rd
Closed Sunday
merci-merci.com

Concept stores don't get much better than this: three floors of French fashion and homewares (think Isabel Marant and Chloé alongside international brands like Levi's and Nike), with a portion of the profits supporting education initiatives in Madagascar. Merci is the most famous spot to shop in the Marais, and the main collections are pricey, but they often showcase new designers—perhaps a cool sunglasses brand or some great totes. Pop-ups might also include collaborations with the likes of household names like Muji and Serax, plus there's a canteen and two cafés onsite. The Used Book Café, where you can browse a 10,000-book-strong library, is particularly cute.

Nouvel Amour

10 rue des Filles du Calvaire, 3rd
Open daily
nouvelamour.fr

Find your new love in jewelry form at this Haut Marais boutique. Founder Delphine Pariente is perhaps best known for her delicate gold-plated medallions, which can be engraved with a word or phrase of your choice—or those of her own design, such as "amour" or "all you need is love." They're hung on long, pendant necklaces or incorporated into simple gold and fabric bracelets. Nouvel Amour's stacking rings, cuffs, quirky earrings, and a small range of leather bags are just as covetable, all elegant but bold. Simpler pieces start at €50.

Papier Tigre

5 rue des Filles du Calvaire, 3rd
Closed Sunday
papiertigre.fr

A must-visit for stationery addicts, Papier Tigre is the place to pick up quirky note cards and notepads, many with their signature geometric, block-color designs. Their minimalist Marais store is a paper treasure-trove for letter writers, doodlers, and diarists. You might also find temporary tattoos, candles, and nail polish, or scarves hand-dyed in Japan, where they have a second store. They even sell wallpaper, although if you're looking for gifts to take home, there are more practical things for your suitcase.

La Super Marquette

65 rue Rambuteau, 4th
Closed Tuesday
lasupermarquette.fr

Amid the souvenir shops clustered around the Centre Pompidou, this one stands out for its classy and original approach. Instead of Eiffel Tower key rings and badly printed aprons mostly made abroad, they stock only French products. The vintage handkerchiefs, brooches, crockery, and cheekily embroidered socks make great gifts. Other items, including tricolore string shopping bags and illustrated maps of the city, might come in useful on your trip. The shop itself is tiny, but they pack a lot into a small space.

CHAPTER 4

The Grands Boulevards

Paris doesn't have a downtown as such, but the Grands Boulevards mark the city's heart. Haussmann's monumental avenues cut elegant swathes through center of Paris, splitting it into myriad smaller neighborhoods, ranging from ritzy shopping districts to once diverse immigrant communities now being transformed by new bars and cafés. It's an area rich in history. Grandiose Second Empire architecture sits alongside art deco cinemas, and medieval towers abut 19th-century arcades.

To the west, Opéra is the hub of theater and the arts in Paris. The elegant colonnades of the Opéra Garnier (France's national opera) are surrounded by high-end hotels and once aristocratic mansions. Just a short walk away you can scoop up bags of designer clothes at Paris's most famous department stores, Printemps and Galeries Lafayette.

Heading east, the area around rue Montorgueil is one of the city's most captivating. Despite being surrounded by new developments, this shopping street has hung on to its traditional roots, still lined with cheese shops, pâtisseries, and greengrocers. It remains a magnet for restaurateurs, too: Grégory Marchand has spawned a mini empire of Frenchie establishments on rue de Nil, while it's just a short walk to superb spots like La Bourse et La Vie for steak-frites. Rue Montmartre, running at a tangent to the northwest, is a good place to go in search of laid-back student bars.

Running off these streets and others nearby are the famous passages, covered arcades that remain just as beautiful as when they were built nearly 200 years ago. Mosaic-floored Galerie Vivienne is the most famous and perhaps the most elegant, but lesser-known arcades like Passage Verdeau are just as spectacular, now filled with secondhand book stalls and independent galleries.

The transition from the 2nd into the 10th arrondissement once marked a transition into less desirable neighborhoods, but the areas around Bonne Nouvelle and Sentier have undergone a huge transformation. Boutique hotels, including an English export, The Hoxton, have moved in alongside smartened-up cafés and cool restaurants. The Faubourg St

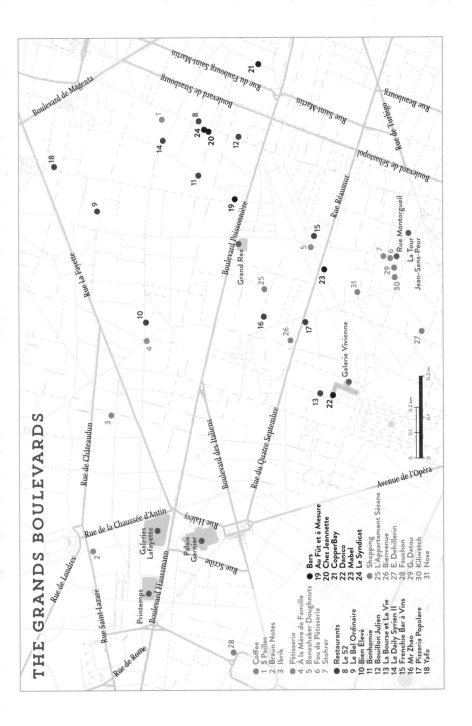

THE GRANDS BOULEVARDS

Coffee
1 5 Pailles
2 Braun Notes
3 Ibrik

Pâtisserie
4 À la Mère de Famille
5 Boneshaker Doughnuts
6 Fou de Pâtisserie
7 Stohrer

Restaurants
8 Le 52
9 Le Bel Ordinaire
10 Bien Élevé
11 Bonhomie
12 Bouillon Julien
13 La Bourse et La Vie
14 Le Daily Syrien II
15 Frenchie Bar à Vins
16 Mr Zhao
17 Pizzeria Popolare
18 Yafo

Bars
19 Au Fût et à Mesure
20 Chez Jeannette
21 CopperBay
22 Danico
23 Mabel
24 Le Syndicat

Shopping
25 L'Appartement Sézane
26 Bienvenue
27 E. Dehillerin
28 Fauchon
29 G. Detou
30 Killiwatch
31 Nose

Denis, located between Gare du Nord and Gare de l'Est, has undergone the most profound change. It was long regarded as the city's seediest quartier, distinguished as a hub of crime and prostitution. Today its shuttered shops are becoming late-night cocktail bars, and family-run Syrian cafés sit alongside New York-inspired all-day dining spots. There are even two triumphal arches, in the same style as the Arc de Triomphe, just next to Strasbourg-Saint-Denis métro.

SEE

Rue Montorgueil

2nd

Until the 1970s—when Les Halles was a sprawling food market rather than an underground mall—shops, bars, and restaurants catering to the hospitality trade spilled out into the surrounding streets. Today few glimpses into this period of history remain, except along and around charming rue Montorgueil, once the main artery bringing goods from the north of France into the city. It remains packed with pavement cafés, greengrocers, butchers, and delis. Strolling this pedestrianized cobbled street is a chance to live, if only for a morning, like the flâneurs of old, idling over a coffee and dipping in and out of nearby arcades like the Passage du Grand-Cerf. Along the way, there are a couple of spots you shouldn't miss: Stohrer, the oldest pâtisserie in Paris, and E.Dehillerin, a temple for cookware geeks.

La Tour Jean-Sans-Peur

20 rue Étienne Marcel, 2nd
Closed Monday and Tuesday

Few medieval buildings remain in Paris, which makes this diminutive tower rather special. It was once part of a larger palace founded by the *ducs de Bourgogne* (Dukes of Burgundy) in the 1200s. The tower itself was built in 1411 and takes its name from the second duc de Bourgogne,

CLOCKWISE FROM TOP LEFT: CHEZ JEANNETTE; RUE DU FAUBOURG ST DENIS; LA TOUR JEAN SANS-PEUR

known as Jean Sans-Peur, who built it to mark his triumph after assassinating his cousin and rival Louis d'Orléans. Today it's less macabre, holding small temporary exhibitions on daily life in the Middle Ages, and you can climb the 140 spiral steps to its upper turret. Don't miss the magnificent stone ceiling carving of entwined oak branches, hops, and hawthorn, each representing a member of the Bourgogne family.

Galerie Vivienne

4 rue des Petits-Champs, 2nd

The most elegant of the passages, Galerie Vivienne was built in 1823 to house local businesses including cobblers, tailors, and wine merchants. You can hardly believe it was left to fall into disrepair and only restored to its original glory in the 1960s. Its beauty appears little faded, the swirling mosaic floor drenched in light pouring in through the glass roof. You can still buy (rather expensive) wine from the esteemed caves of Legrand Filles et Fils, while traditional trades have been replaced by fancy jewelers, leather goods stores, and a superb cocktail bar, Danico.

Palais Garnier

Place de l'Opéra, 9th
Open daily

The jewel of the Opéra National de Paris, who also stage productions at the Opéra Bastille, the Palais Garnier was completed after 17 years of construction in 1875—at the time becoming the 13th opera house in the city. Tickets for a show start around an eye-watering €100, but it costs around just €10 to visit on a tour. The interior is magnificent, almost rivaling some of the state rooms at Versailles with its glitzy Grand Foyer (in fact inspired by Versailles' Hall of Mirrors), imposing staircase, and chandelier-lit hallways. The main auditorium itself even has a ceiling painting by Chagall, added in the 1960s. Time your trip early or late in the day to avoid the crowds.

Galeries Lafayette

40 boulevard Haussmann, 9th
Open daily
galerieslafayette.com

You don't need to love shopping to fall in love with Galeries Lafayette, famed not just for its stable of luxury brands, but its simply magical 43-metre-high stained-glass dome that soars above the main atrium. From humble beginnings as a luxury bazaar in 1912, the store has grown to span three sites on boulevard Haussmann: the main store Lafayette Coupole, Lafayette Maison and Gourmet (homewares and food), and Lafayette Homme (menswear). The collections are continually expanding, but Chanel, Hermès, Longchamp, and Saint Laurent are just a few of the names you can expect to find as you explore. If you're lucky enough to be in Paris around Christmas, this is one of the best times to visit Galeries Lafayette: they go all out with lights, Christmas trees, and window displays.

Printemps

64 boulevard Haussmann, 9th
Open daily
printemps.com

The other Grands Boulevards department store grande dame, Printemps, is just down the road from Galeries Lafayette, and the two are easy to visit as a pair. The store opened a little earlier than Galleries Lafayette, in 1865. Printemps, following in the footsteps of the 1852 opening of Le Bon Marché on the Left Bank, has since never stopped expanding. Today you can browse extensive men's, women's, and children's ranges as well as what's claimed to be the largest beauty department in the world. The latest addition is Perruche, a chic cocktail bar and restaurant atop Printemps de l'Homme, which offers stupendous views across the city.

Overwhelmed by the range of shops in Paris and the amount of goods on offer in the grands magasins? Start simple and focus on picking up these five essentials that you'll love and use long after you get home.

A Breton tee: An essential for a reason, blue-and-white striped Breton T-shirts are the unisex staple everyone should have in their wardrobe. The design, first introduced as part of the French navy uniform in the late 1800s, was later popularized by Coco Chanel. Traditionally, the white stripes are double the width of the blue.

Sunglasses: Despite the fact that Paris enjoys around just 200 days of sunshine each year, sunglasses are de rigueur to sit outdoors with a morning coffee. As well as big-name labels, there's an ever-growing range of indie brands that make one-of-a-kind styles each season.

Skin care: Embrace the French pharmacy skin care cult and pick up a La Roche-Posay moisturizer or a Klorane oat milk shampoo. You might be able to find these brands online—but you can't beat the range and price of the products on offer in most corner drugstores in Paris.

Scented candles: Finding the right home fragrance is just as important as choosing your signature scent. Pick a Paris-inspired perfume or one made with French botanicals and you'll have a long-lasting reminder of your trip.

Scarves: It's a bit of a running joke that Parisians even carry a scarf in summer, but the truth is you can find really beautiful écharpes and foulards throughout the year. The former usually refers to weightier winter scarves, perhaps in a delicate wool knit; while the latter covers lighter silks, such as those made famous by Hermès.

Le Grand Rex

1 boulevard Poissonnière, 2nd

legrandrex.com

Going to see a movie in a language you don't speak might not be the most obvious thing to do on vacation, but Paris and cinema have a special connection. Le Grand Rex is the largest cinema in Europe, built in 1932, and its grande salle is an art deco delight. You can see it in all its glory on one of their irregular two-hour tours (check the website) or simply book tickets for a screening. Look out for international movies listed as VOST (*version originale sous-titrée*) and you'll get the original audio with no dubbing as well as French subtitles if you want to test your language skills.

COFFEE

5 Pailles

79 rue du Faubourg Saint-Denis, 10th

Open daily

5pailles.com

What looks like a teeny coffee bar with a few outside tables at the slightly more run-down end of rue du Faubourg Saint-Denis is actually a superb lunch and brunch spot. They offer much more than just your specialty coffee fix. Yes, you can order a long black with a slice of vegan pear crumble to go, but slip past the bar and you'll discover a cozy dining room. Here they serve everything from chia pudding and granola to *tartines* (open sandwiches), pancakes, and eggs benedict all day long. At lunchtime it's just €12 for their formule: a main dish with a soft drink or black coffee of your choice.

Braun Notes

31–33 rue de Mogador, 9th
Open daily

AeroPress addicts, rejoice. Braun Notes has you covered after a shopping binge at Printemps or Galeries Lafayette. It's a small shop, decked out in wood-and-copper, with a couple of street tables in summer. Their juices and hot chocolates are also worth a stop-off, although at the weekend things get slightly ridiculous with granola brunch bowls served in half coconuts and cutesy latte art. During the week you can snack on chai cakes, cookies, and chocolate-date cake.

Ibrik

43 rue Laffitte, 9th
Closed Sunday
ibrik.fr

This coffee shop offers something a little bit different. Calling themselves "Byzantino disruptive," they serve a light Middle-Eastern–inspired menu of mezze, shakshuka, pitas, and salads along with coffee. Their name comes from the *ibrik,* also sometimes called a *cezve,* the copper pot used to brew thick, sweet Turkish-style coffee, which you can order here as well as the usual third-wave espressos, pour-overs, and the like. Save room for chocolate halva cookies, sticky pistachio cakes, and Valrhona chocolate fondants to finish. Lighter options include Greek yogurt bowls with dried apricots and nuts.

PÂTISSERIE

À la Mère de Famille

35 rue du Faubourg Montmartre, 9th
Open daily
lameredefamille.com

The most gorgeously old-fashioned chocolate shop, À la Mère de Famille has been in business since 1761 and making confectionery since 1856. This shop is somewhat of a time warp, both outside, where gold lettering covers nearly every inch of its dark green façade, and inside where you can pick up boxes of *orangettes* (crystalized orange strips coated in dark chocolate), *marrons glacés* (candied chestnuts), and pots of *pâtes à tartiner* (decadent chocolate spreads). Other beautifully packaged gifts include pralines, marshmallows, and chocolate-coated almonds. They're renowned for their seasonal displays, so be sure to stop by if you're visiting around Easter and Christmas—or even Halloween.

Boneshaker Doughnuts

77 rue d'Aboukir, 2nd
Closed Sunday and Monday
boneshakerparis.com

Great doughnuts are no longer impossible to find in Paris thanks to Amanda Bankert and Louis Scott's bakery, Boneshaker Doughnuts. They've developed a huge following for their classics—some with a French twist, like salted butter caramel—their seasonal specials, and their super-friendly service. Wash down combinations like peanut butter and sea salt, chocolate and stout, or candied walnuts and lime with one of their strong-but-smooth filter coffees, made with beans from Belleville Brûlerie.

Fou de Pâtisserie

45 rue Montorgueil, 2nd
Open daily
foudepatisserieboutique.fr

This teeny concept store is all about the next big thing. Owners Julie Mathieu and Muriel Tallandier, editors of a magazine of the same name as their store, sell treats from some of the city's leading pâtissiers—and were the first to bring multiple talents under the same roof. Some creations may look familiar, such as Angelina's "altesse" (a shortbread biscuit topped with vanilla ganache and raspberries) or Pierre Marcolini's caramel and pistachio chocolate bars. Others are less expected, like Catherine Kluger's chocolate granola and Gilles Marchal's orange-flower marshmallows.

Stohrer

51 rue Montorgueil, 2nd
Open daily
stohrer.fr

The city's oldest pâtisserie, founded in 1730, Stohrer is a bastion of tradition and an institution like no other. This is where the *baba au rhum* (a dense doughnut-like cake drenched in rum), was created. As well as the obligatory baba, you can pick up obscenely light madeleines, caramel-laced millefeuilles, seasonal fruit tartlets, and specials like miniature croissants stuffed with sweet raspberry confit. Their savory delicacies are also popular; look out for everything from cheesy quiches to puff pastry tomato swirls.

RESTAURANTS

Le 52

52 rue du Faubourg Saint-Denis, 10th
Open daily
faubourgstdenis.com

Nowhere else shows quite how much the Faubourg Saint-Denis has gentrified as Le 52. Not only is this one of the rare restaurants in Paris to be open from 8 a.m. through to midnight, albeit with the full menu only served at lunch and dinner, they also run a strict no-reservations policy. The aesthetic wouldn't be out of place in New York: plenty of buzzy bar seats and a sleek, almost Scandi-style decor. International influences are less evident on the menu, with the food firmly modern French in style. Dishes change daily but might include combinations like veal carpaccio with cucumber, or duck breast with cranberry and pistachio. It's incredible value for the quality, too, at around €20 for a main dish.

Le Bel Ordinaire

54 rue de Paradis, 10th
Closed Sunday and Monday
lebelordinaire.com

There's only one problem with natural wine bars in Paris: They tend to be small, cramped, and occasionally unwelcoming to English speakers not familiar with the difference between pét-nat and Pouilly-Fuissé. This delightfully airy and modern cave, épicerie, and restaurant is the antidote. Well off the established wine-enthusiast tourist trail, it's at once a deli, wine shop, and laid-back restaurant. Come with an open mind. You could snack on burrata laced with raspberry purée with a glass of Riesling from Azay-le-Rideau, or you could try radishes drenched in butter and salt with a Cabernet Franc from the Loire. It's the kind of place you stop for a glass and snack and end up wobbling out several glasses and small plates later.

Bien Élevé

47 rue Richer, 9th
Closed Sunday and Monday
bieneleve.fr

Simple decor matches the simple philosophy at Bien Élevé, where a short menu puts sustainably sourced, quality meat and fish reared in France front and center. There's not a lot of choice—a burger, a catch of the day, a steak, all for less than €25—but everything is cooked with skill and presented with style. Add-ons include béarnaise sauce and beef dripping fries, plus there are some simple starters like terrines and soups. If you've still got room, move on to the cheese plate, a pistachio financier, or a brownie drizzled with salted butter caramel for dessert.

Bonhomie

22 rue d'Enghien, 10th
Open daily until late
bonhomie.paris

This glorious restaurant might just have the best bar seats in the city. First there's the bar itself, where you can pull up a padded wooden stool and sip a beautifully made cocktail, then there's the slab of a marble bar countertop that gives around 10 diners an up-close view into the open kitchen. Think Paris meets *Mad Men,* with a constantly changing seasonal Mediterranean menu that'll always give you a reason to return: perhaps pollack with cauliflower and fennel, or heritage tomatoes served deceptively

BONHOMIE

simply with kalamata olives and feta. You could even just eat the *mezze*, making a meal out of Iberian ham and za'atar topped mozzarella.

Bouillon Julien

16 rue du Faubourg Saint-Denis, 10th
Open daily
bouillon-julien.com

Founded in 1906, and completely revamped in 2018, Bouillon Julien joins a citywide revival of art nouveau brasseries. The mirrored dining room is simply beautiful: sea green walls, intricate paneling, and a magnificent mahogany bar. Édith Piaf and her lover, boxer Marcel Cerdan, are said to have regularly dined at table 24. In keeping with its history, it also remains one of the most affordable places to eat in the area—plats start at just €10 and some desserts are less than €3. Embrace the super-traditional with *poireaux vinaigrette* (dressed leeks), followed by an endive and ham gratin, and prune clafoutis to finish.

La Bourse et La Vie

12 rue Vivienne, 2nd
Closed Saturday and Sunday
labourselavie.com

Opened by one of the best-known American chefs in Paris, Daniel Rose, La Bourse et La Vie's smart take on the Parisian bistro is hard to beat. This compact spot is unsurprisingly popular with diners from both sides of the Atlantic, who come to spend around €40 for a plate of superb steak-frites with *sauce poivre* (pepper sauce), their signature dish. Also on the short menu are duck *à l'Alsacienne* (with roasted foie gras) and a superb pig's head terrine. Just note that there's little, if anything, for those of a vegetarian persuasion.

Le Daily Syrien II

12 rue des Petites Écuries, 10th
Closed Sunday

In the mood for authentic mezze? Head to Le Daily Syrien II, sister restaurant to the take-out spot of the same name on rue du Faubourg Saint-Denis. The vibe is laid-back and low-key, perfect for over-ordering plate after plate of labneh, falafel, moussaka, and *moutabal* (eggplant caviar), all for around €6 each. There are also various shawarmas, feta salads, and formules for just €15. If you're not familiar with Syrian food, it's well worth a stop. To drink there's Lebanese wine from Château Kefraya, as well as beers, teas, and fresh juices.

Frenchie Bar à Vins

6 rue du Nil, 2nd
Daily from 6 p.m.
frenchie-bav.com

Grégory Marchand's empire continues to grow. In the past 10 years he's become one of the best-known chefs on the Paris restaurant scene, adopting the nickname Frenchie (given to him by Jamie Oliver during his time at Fifteen in London) as his hallmark. Frenchie Bar à Vins was his second project and remains the best spot to get a taste of his cooking and ethos. There are no reservations and little space, but superb wines and snacks—think homemade terrines and rillettes complemented by cheeses from London's Neal's Yard Dairy. The extensive by-the-glass wine menu changes regularly, so you could find yourself sipping an elegant red Burgundy or discovering a unique Chardonnay aged *sous voile* (under a film of yeast; it tastes a bit like sherry). Across the road is the reservation-only Frenchie restaurant proper (tasting menus from around €80) and takeout joint Frenchie To Go, where you can pick up an incongruous mix of English scones and New York–style reubens and hot dogs.

Mr Zhao

37 rue des Jeûneurs, 2nd
Closed Sunday
mrzhao.fr

Stop by Mr Zhao for Xi'an-style street food in the heart of the 2nd arrondissement. Start with fried chicken dumplings or the Shaanxi specialty *rou jia mo,* here just called mo (a squidgy bun filled with slow-cooked pork, tofu, or duck). The main event is biang biang noodles, customized with the toppings of your choice (around €12), ideally accompanied by a Tsingtao beer. It's not a spot to settle in for the evening—much of the kitchen's work is fulfilling delivery orders—but it's one of the most enjoyable spots for regional Chinese cuisine in the center of the city.

Pizzeria Popolare

111 rue Réaumur, 2nd
Daily lunch and dinner
bigmammagroup.com

Pizza is ubiquitous in Paris. Good pizza is not, which goes some way to explain the hype surrounding Big Mamma Group's tribute to all things Neapolitan, an enormous restaurant seating 250 by Sentier métro. It's cheap, good, and crazily popular. The €5 margarita might be stuff of legend, but there's plenty more besides. Sink your teeth into a Red Hot Burrata (pizza topped with burrata, spicy salami, and zucchini flowers) or a la norma di lello (pizza topped with fried eggplant, mint, and lime zest). House cocktails kick off at around €6, and if you get carried away, the basement turns into a club from Thursday to Sunday.

Yafo

96 rue d'Hauteville, 10th
Closed Saturday and Sunday
yafo-restaurant.com

Don't be put off by the limited lunchtime-only weekday hours, this smart white-tiled café is an essential stop if you're hankering for some hummus (made here with tahini imported from Israel). Choose between plain hummus sprinkled with cumin and smoked paprika, or go for one of their daily meat or veggie toppings, order some cauliflower tabbouleh or salad on the side, and then tear up your pitta bread and get eating. Up the spice with pickles and homemade harissa, or save room for *malabi* (a rosewater milk pudding) for dessert. Expect to spend around €20 a head.

BARS

Au Fût et à Mesure

2 rue d'Hauteville, 10th
Closed Sunday

A beer bar with a difference, at Au Fût et à Mesure you don't order your drinks, but pour them yourself. Thanks to a clever prepay card system, you choose your on-tap beer from self-service pumps on each table—although there are bartender-made cocktails as well if you're not a fan of their latest IPA or Belgian Blond. When there's not a game on, the music is loud and the atmosphere is lively, with booze-balancing snacks like saucisson, cheese plates, and bread and hummus.

Chez Jeannette

47 rue du Faubourg Saint-Denis, 10th
Daily 9 a.m. to 2 a.m.

Rue du Faubourg Saint-Denis might still straddle the delicate line between super cool and super seedy, but this corner bar was one of the first places to start the road's transformation. Even when it's packed at night with drinkers spilling out onto the street, it retains something of a scruffy elegance. During the day expect the pace—and service—to be slow. Draw up one of the red leather chairs at a scuffed Formica table, order an espresso, and take in the original features: high ceilings with beautiful moldings and a copper-edged bar, now illuminated by CHEZ JEANNETTE spelled out in neon lettering above. Drinks are similarly unfussy: basic coffees, a handful of beers on tap, spirits and wines by the glass.

CHEZ JEANNETTE

CopperBay

5 rue Bouchardon, 10th
Closed Sunday and Monday
copperbay.fr

With a vibe that's intended to be more yacht club bar than secret speakeasy, this quirky cocktail spot is light, bright, and fun. Transport yourself to the south of France and sip a pastis or try one of their original creations (from €12) like the julep-style O Perfume with gin, white port, and tarragon. The menu changes seasonally, so there's always something new to try, and they don't take themselves too seriously: Stencil designs on frothy cocktails might include lips, stars, or even Toad from Mario Kart.

Danico

6 rue Vivienne, 2nd
Daily 6 p.m. to 2 a.m.

It's rare to find a cocktail bar with a reputation that surpasses the restaurant it adjoins. Danico, attached to Italian restaurant Daroco, is such a bar. This location has always been a stylish spot—it was once Jean Paul Gaultier's Galerie Vivienne boutique. Danico has continued the design spirit of the place with kitschy but classy green velvet chairs and a striped marble bar topped with glinting gold barware. They welcome visiting bartenders, and their drink list shows plenty of international inspiration. You could find yourself sipping a Kung Fu Pandan (whisky, saké, PX, soy sauce, peach bitters, and vermouth infused with pandan leaves) or a Rock Shisor Paper (shochu infused with shiso leaves, cherry blossom cordial, and grapefruit zest).

Mabel

58 rue d'Aboukir, 2nd
Closed Sunday
mabelparis.com

Step into rum wonderland. All spirits were not created equal in the eyes of Mabel founder Joseph Akhavan, hence the invention of this cocktail bar. They stock more than 100 rums from Belize to Madagascar and serve them alongside gourmet grilled cheese sandwiches (an underrated and perhaps never before perfected combination). Expand your horizons with a rum flight or try one of their cocktails for around €15—the Italian Job (Smith & Cross rum with Aperol, Byrrh Grand Quinquina, and Cocchi Americano) is a great place to start if you like your drinks strong and bitter.

Le Syndicat

51 rue du Faubourg Saint-Denis, 10th
Open daily
syndicatcocktailclub.com

If you visit one cocktail bar in Paris, make it this one. You could easily miss its unsigned façade, papered in layers of tatty flyers, and you'd be forgiven for assuming it was a dive bar or even an abandoned shop. Yet inside it's a temple to a new style of mixology. They stock only French spirits, which they use in original creations and twists on classic cocktails. Try specials like Biggie Smalls Door (featuring the Corsican aperitif Cap Mattei and grapefruit cordial) or La Voix de Mickey, served with a balloon of cotton candy-flavored helium (which you inhale to embody the cocktail's name, the voice of Mickey Mouse). The hip-hop soundtrack might be loud and the walls covered in graffiti, but the second you sit down it will be clear that although staff and drinkers alike are here to have fun, service is taken seriously. Stay until they close and you might just find yourself doodling on the walls and being given free shots of Blanche de Normandie before you stumble home.

SHOPPING

L'Appartement Sézane

1 rue Saint-Fiacre, 2nd
Closed Sunday and Monday

No other brand has managed to capitalize on making once unattainable French-girl cool accessible like Sézane. From floaty summer dresses and throw-on knitwear to flared jeans and elegant wrap skirts, their limited seasonal collections are eye-catching yet simple; fashion-forward yet flattering. Prices, at around €150 for a dress or €100 for a pair of jeans, are aspirational but not unaffordable. With the cult status of some pieces—there was once a 30,000-person waiting list for the Barry cardigan—it's little wonder the company is quickly expanding in France and abroad. They started as an online-only brand, and L'Appartement was their first brick-and-mortar showcase.

Bienvenue

7 rue d'Hauteville, 10th
Closed Sunday
bienvenuestore.com

A concept store with a rare masculine aesthetic, Bienvenue seamlessly blends old-school luxury brands with contemporary street style in a small but cool space just off boulevard de Bonne Nouvelle. Somehow both English-made Hunter rain boots and Helmut Lang cologne seem at home here, as do Eastpak backpacks, Sigg water bottles, and Off-White high tops. They stock a limited range, but everything is exceptionally well chosen, ready to slot straight into a Parisian capsule wardrobe. Look out for accessories from up-and-coming French designers, too: perhaps a Maison Baluchon bag, Maison Lip watch, or Commune de Paris tee.

E.Dehillerin

18–20 rue Coquillière, 1st
Closed Sunday

Amateur cooks and chefs alike have been shopping at E.Dehillerin for nearly two centuries. Paul Bocuse and Julia Child have sung its praises, and Anthony Bourdain even picked up a duck press here on his series, *The Layover*. Yes, it's old school. But it's also a gold mine for budding gourmands, crammed with every kind of mold, knife, and dish you can imagine. Whether you're looking for a beautiful copper pan, smaller items like whisks, spatulas, and pastry cutters, or something more niche like a fish kettle or fondue set, you won't leave empty-handed.

Fauchon

30 place de la Madeleine, 8th
Closed Sunday
fauchon.com

It's been more than 130 years since Auguste Fauchon opened his first deli on this spot. The brand has since grown to span two buildings, covering nearly

5,000 square feet, and become a household name in France and beyond. These days the Fauchon empire even includes a five-star hotel, but their Madeleine emporium remains a delightful place to come in search of gourmet gifts. Conserves, oils, and jars of pâté and jam are some of the best things to take home, or you can stop by the bakery (24–26 place de la Madeleine) for a box of their macarons, claimed by many to be among the best in Paris.

G. Detou

58 rue Tiquetonne, 2nd
Closed Sunday

Once you've stocked up on cookware at E.Dehillerin, you can't leave without stopping by G. Detou for ingredients. This celebrated store specializes in high-quality pâtisserie supplies: Valrhona chocolate, dried fruits, fine cocoa, candied flowers, pistachio paste, marrons glacés, and many more things you never knew you needed but simply must buy. On the savory side there are mustards, oils, spices, tins of sardines, pâtés, and pickles. It's a great spot for gifts, but an even better one to source ingredients to re-create a dish you've tried.

Kiliwatch

64 rue Tiquetonne, 2nd
Closed Sunday
kiliwatch.paris

Kiliwatch is all about retro, mixing mini-ranges from cool Parisian and international designers with a simply enormous vintage collection. Come with at least an hour to spare to rummage through the slightly chaotic racks. Whether your style is streetwear or something a little more chic, there's sure to be something hiding for you. On the thrift side of things you could pick up anything from a Ralph Lauren tea dress to a bargain shearling aviator jacket, while the contemporary collections feature the likes of Grace & Mila's tough-yet-feminine designs and Japanese-inspired denim from Canadian brand Naked & Famous.

Nose

20 rue Bachaumont, 2nd
Closed Sunday
nose.fr

There's only one way to pick your Parisian fragrance: with an olfactive diagnostic at Nose. In their sleek showroom-meets-modern-day apothecary, they'll give you five recommendations based on your personal perfume preferences. First you'll be directed toward the most suitable of seven fragrance categories (floral, citrus, oriental, floriental, chypre, fougere, woody), and then be given a hand-selected range of their 500 or so perfumes and colognes to try. They might also introduce you to some new concepts like fragrance filters, which you can layer on top of your favorite scent to strengthen its intensity or bring out different notes.

CHAPTER 5

Montmartre, Pigalle, and SoPi

In search of ivy-draped balconies, candle-lit restaurants, and seemingly endless city vistas? Montmartre has them all. This is the most atmospheric part of Paris, a tangle of cobbled streets winding down and around the steep slopes of the Butte Montmartre, the majestic white basilica of the Sacré-Cœur perched on the hilltop above. Montmartre and romance go hand in hand. Boutique-hotel boltholes abound, as do peaceful gardens and quiet squares where you can stroll with your amour (or maybe several amoureux—this was once one of the most bohemian quartiers after all). As the sun sets and sightseers head off elsewhere, there's no better place to get a little bit lost and see where you end up.

The Sacré-Cœur is Montmartre's crowning glory. This Roman Catholic church is very much in regular use today, and climbing the 222 steps to its door still feels like an act of pilgrimage. The views over Paris are simply spectacular: a dense carpet of rooftops only punctuated by the Eiffel Tower in the west, Tour Montparnasse in the south, and the hills of Buttes-Chaumont in the east. It's lucky that stopping to take pictures is a good excuse to catch your breath during the climb. During the day these steps are a forest of selfie-sticks and camera tripods. After dark, they often play host to an impromptu international party as music blares from phones, joints are passed around, and wine is shared from plastic cups.

Around the Sacré-Cœur at the top of the Butte, the streets are filled with businesses cashing in on the tourist trade. The most famous spot is Place du Tertre, a sort of faux country town square crammed with overpriced bistros as well as artists and cartoonists plying their trade. Similarly at the Butte's base, the tat hawked along rue de Dunkerque is truly staggering. If you want an Eiffel Tower–branded shot glass, phone cover, or even boxer briefs, this is where to come.

Take the time to explore a little farther, and in the space of a few streets the atmosphere changes. Local tabacs and bars replace touts. Hotels and hostels are outnumbered by elegant mansions and classical apartment blocks. Souvenir stands are swapped with super-cute concept stores.

MONTMARTRE, PIGALLE, AND SOPI

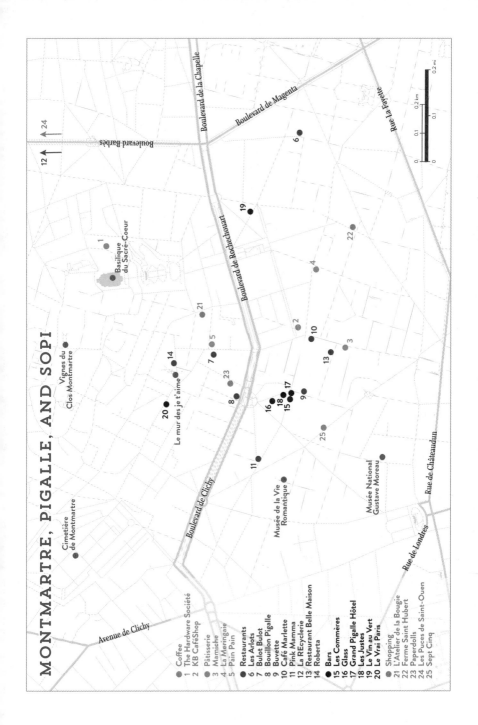

Coffee
1 The Hardware Société
2 KB CaféShop

Pâtisserie
3 Mamiche
4 La Meringaïe
5 Pain Pain

Restaurants
6 Les Arlots
7 Bulot Bulot
8 Bouillon Pigalle
9 Buvette
10 Café Marlette
11 Pink Mamma
12 La REcyclerie
13 Restaurant Belle Maison
14 Roberta

Bars
15 Les Commères
16 Glass
17 Grand Pigalle Hôtel
18 Les Justes
19 Le Vin au Vert
20 Le Vrai Paris

Shopping
21 L'Atelier de la Bougie
22 Ferme Saint Hubert
23 Paperdolls
24 Les Puces de Saint-Ouen
25 Sept Cinq

Café-lined roads such as rue des Abbesses are particularly pretty, while rue du Mont-Cenis has the best views to the north. Maurice Utrillo—whose works you can see in the Orangerie—famously painted them from his window in the early 1900s. More unusual is Villa Léandre, a street just off avenue Junot lined with English-style houses. You should also look out for beautiful street art (check out the flamingos on rue Berthe) and charming gardens like Square Jehan Rictus, where you'll find *le mur des je t'aime* (The Wall of Love). Just five minutes walk from Place du Tertre, there's even an entire vineyard hidden on the Butte's northern flank.

The area south of the boulevard de Clichy, now dubbed SoPi (south of Pigalle), couldn't be more different. In just a few years it's gone from being Paris's seedy red-light district to one of the coolest places to go for a night out. There's still the odd sex shop and strip club, but they're now far out-numbered by *bobos* (bourgeois bohemians, Paris's own brand of hipster) who come here for cocktail bars and brunches. Much of the action is along rue Frochot, where American-inspired late-night bar Glass led the way before being joined by classy cocktail spots like Les Justes. Southeast of here, rue des Martyrs has a much more laid-back vibe and is the place to come for a quiet coffee or a lunch en terrasse.

SEE

Basilique du Sacré-Cœur

Parvis du Sacré-Cœur, 18th
Open daily
sacre-coeur-montmartre.com

The Sacré-Cœur is visible from many points across the city, the smooth curves of its Byzantine-inspired domes at odds with the Gothic spires and flying buttresses that characterize many French cathedrals. Architectur-ally it has more in common with Saint Mark's Basilica in Venice than it does most religious monuments in France. The first stone was laid here in 1875, but the church opened much later in 1919 after the outbreak of

CLOCKWISE FROM THE TOP: THE SACRÉ-CŒUR; RUE DU MONT-CENIS; MONTMARTRE STREET VIEW

World War I delayed its completion. Its interior is just as magnificent as the views from its steps, the ceiling of the apse covered in an intricate gold mosaic and its side chapels lit by hundreds of flickering candles. At any time of day people are often at prayer, and the atmosphere is hushed and reverential. Note that if you want (or need) to skip the stairs to get here, métro tickets are valid on the funicular that runs from Place Saint-Pierre almost to the Basilica's entrance.

Vignes du Clos Montmartre

Rue des Saules, 18th
Visits by appointment only

Montmartre is full of surprises, but none are quite as memorable as discovering a working vineyard just a few hundred meters from the Sacré-Cœur. The Vignes du Clos Montmartre, set at the top of the Butte's northern slope just as it starts to fall away toward Lamarck-Caulaincourt, is home to the oldest vines in Paris. Few stumble upon it by accident, making this one of the city's best-kept secrets. The only downside is that you can't just walk in for a stroll. Montmartre's tourist office offers oenologist-guided tours for large groups or you can

THE FÊTE DES VENDANGES DE MONTMARTE

get access as part of a handful of food and wine experiences sold through Viator (viator.com). If you're lucky enough to be in Paris around harvest time (usually October) you could also join in with the annual three-day festival, the Fête des Vendanges de Montmartre, held here since 1934. The 1,000 or so bottles produced each year, considered "unicorn wines" for their rarity, are only available to buy around festival time.

Cimetière de Montmartre

20 avenue Rachel, 18th

Open daily

Père Lachaise might be Paris's most famous cemetery—and the world's most visited—but it's not the only one worth exploring in Paris. The Cimetière de Montmartre has its own fascinating history. Officially known as the Cimetière du Nord, it was opened in 1825 on the site of a more ancient burial ground, and it still retains a little of the quiet, park-like atmosphere it must have once had before the city expanded around its perimeters. Today you can stroll the cobbled pathways or look over them from above as you walk the Pont de Caulaincourt, a bridge built over the cemetery in the late 1800s. The roll call of famous burials (if you're into paying respects to stars now departed) includes singer and icon Dalida, who lived nearby and whose grave is often covered with fresh flowers, celebrated Impressionist painter Degas, and composer Joseph Kosma. Free maps will help you find your way around.

Le mur des je t'aime

Square Jehan Rictus, 18th

Love isn't in the air in Square Jehan Rictus, it's written on the wall. This tiny garden just by Abbesses métro now attracts lovers and selfie-takers from around the world who flock to see Frédéric Baron and Claire Kito's masterful mural, which adorns its cracked, vine-covered western wall. *Le mur des je t'aime* is a 100-square-foot artwork comprising more than 600 navy-blue tiles across on which "I love you" is written in 250 languages. Scattered between the text are seemingly random red geometric shapes that, if rearranged, would form a heart. Whether you want to say "te amo," "te iubesc," "au domoni iko," or "saya cinta padamu," this Montmartre monument is not to be missed.

Musée de la Vie Romantique

16 rue Chaptal, 9th

Closed Monday

museevieromantique.paris.fr

Down a little alleyway south of Pigalle, in a quartier sometimes known as Nouvelle Athènes, this one-of-a-kind museum occupies a family house built in 1830. Owned by Ary Scheffer, it became a hub of the artistic scene of the time, visited by Chopin, Delacroix, and most significantly George Sand, whose furniture and personal memorabilia are displayed on the ground floor. You won't get much insight into the personal life of the great writer (who is said to have had numerous passionate affairs, including one with Chopin and another with the poet Alfred Musset), but her trinkets and family paintings evoke the spirit of an era that's rarely preserved. Upstairs there's beautiful portraiture and works owned by the Scheffer-Renan family, who donated the house to the state to be opened as a museum in the 1950s. The garden has now been turned into a peaceful courtyard café, the perfect spot for a secluded cup of coffee and slice of cake.

Musée National Gustave Moreau

14 rue de la Rochefoucauld, 9th

Closed Tuesday

musee-moreau.fr

Exploring small single-artist museums is one of the joys of sightseeing in Paris. Rather than being overwhelmed by hundreds of works spanning various movements and styles, you can get an insight into the artistic process of just one painter. Musée National Gustave Moreau, in the home and studio of the symbolist painter, is among the best of its ilk—conceived as a museum by the artist himself. There are nearly 4,000 works to discover here, including *Jupiter et Sémélé*, considered his chef d'oeuvre. Even the spiral staircase connecting the studio to his personal rooms is a masterpiece in itself.

MUSSÉE DE LA VIE ROMANTIQUE

The Hardware Société

10 rue Lamarck, 18th

Closed Tuesday and Wednesday

This Australian import in the shadow of the Sacré-Cœur might pride itself on no reservations or collaborations, but that's done nothing to quell its popularity. They're usually open until around 4 p.m., but the expat-heavy crowd is really here for the breakfasts: smooth espressos served with tiny bite-sized beignets, pork belly with potato and bacon hash, lobster eggs benedict, and brioche French toast. Service can be slow, but it's the perfect antidote to the Disneyfied faux-French cafés that cluster in nearby Place du Tertre. Skip the croissants, though; this isn't the best spot for pâtisserie.

KB CaféShop

53 avenue Trudaine, 9th

Open daily

Self-proclaimed roasters, brewers, and cake makers, the team behind KB CaféShop have created a laid-back and light-filled café at the top of rue des Martyrs. The bar is always loaded with baked goods, from cakes and brownies to English-style scones and sandwiches, and they sell bags of their in-house-roasted beans to take away. It's a lovely spot in summer, when tables extend onto the sidewalk to make the most of their coveted corner location, but can be a bit crowded inside if you're looking for a spot to set up your laptop or read a book.

PÂTISSERIE

Mamiche

45 rue Condorcet, 9th
Closed Sunday
mamiche.fr

Low-key and untraditional, Mamiche is a neighborhood boulangerie reinvented. Their sugar-dusted beignets (doughnuts by another name), chocolate cookies, and financiers are just what you need to sate a serious sweet-tooth craving, while their beautifully flaky croissants and pains au chocolat can't be bettered in this quartier. At lunch they package up just-filled baguettes with a drink and dessert, making Mamiche the perfect one-stop shop if you want lunch on the go. Look out for specials like orange blossom brioche and cinnamon scrolls.

La Meringaie

35 rue des Martyrs, 9th
Closed Monday
lameringaie.com

Bakeries doing one thing and doing it well are a Parisian specialty. On the menu at La Meringaie? Meringues, of course, topped pavlova-style with mounds of whipped cream and fresh fruit. Seasonal specials at their minimalist rue des Martyrs boutique (they have two others in Paris) might include a chocolate cream with pear or a tropical coconut cream with kiwi and mango. Full-size versions are best shared between four or five people for dessert; their individual meringues are the perfect solo afternoon treat.

CLOCKWISE FROM TOP LEFT: BOUILLON PIGALLE; BULOT BULOT; MAMICHE; HARDWARE SOCIÉTÉ

Pain Pain

88 rue des Martyrs, 18th
Closed Monday
pain-pain.fr

It's been a few years since Pain Pain scooped the award for the best baguette in Paris, but this corner bakery certainly hasn't rested on its laurels. You should definitely come for the breads and brioche, but pâtissier Sébastien Mauvieux is also a dab hand when it comes to sweeter delicacies, from American inspired brownies topped with pecan Chantilly cream to classic millefeuilles and cinnamon chaussons aux pommes. Their Instagram is a thing of beauty, mixing pictures of their latest creations with snaps of their graphic-print paper bags brightening up picnics across Paris. There are, however, a few seats to perch on if you don't want to eat on the go.

RESTAURANTS

Les Arlots

136 rue du Faubourg Poissonnière, 10th
Closed Sunday and Monday

This friendly backstreet bistro has raked in awards, not for fancy cooking but by reintroducing honest, old-fashioned dishes without pretension. They've repopularized *pot au feu* (a classic beef stew), *brandade de morue* (salt-cod gratin), and their signature, *saucisse purée* (sausage and mash). Even better, you can get two courses for around €20 at lunch and there are more than 100 organic wines to choose from to accompany your meal. It's an unexpected find near Gare du Nord, and it's the kind of place you could happily take a date or your Grandma. Just come hungry: portions are generous.

Bulot Bulot

83 rue des Martyrs, 18th
Closed Monday, evenings only Tuesday–Friday
bulotbulot.fr

A fishermen's shack is the last thing you'd expect to find in Montmartre, but this neon-lit, wood-clad micro-restaurant is a fun, modern take on a traditional bar à huîtres. Come to pair oysters and with a spritz at the bar, or jostle for space at a table to snack on marinated anchovies, truffle tarama, or smoked red mullet. If you want something a bit less, er, fishy, they also serve lobster and crab rolls. For dessert they offer key lime pie and chocolate fondant.

Bouillon Pigalle

22 boulevard de Clichy, 18th
Open daily
bouillonpigalle.com

Bouillons, cheap and cheerful brasseries, flourished in Paris during the Belle Époque. It's said that an enterprising butcher who found he could use his off-cuts in meaty soups—known as bouillons—and sell them at rock-bottom prices established the first "bouillon" near Les Halles. By the turn of the 20th century, there were more than 250 now-lost bouillons across the city. Bouillon Pigalle has reinvented this great tradition for a new generation, with a menu of *escargots* (snails), *os à moelle* (bone marrow), and steak served in a super-cool location in the 18th. It's quality food yet very affordable: You can get two courses with a drink or two for less than €20. There's no wine list, just two reds, two whites, and a rosé available in sizes from the mini carafe (250ml) to the jeroboam (3 liters)—great fun if you're in a group, if impossible to pour. They've also introduced two new concepts: no reservations and queuing. Although the restaurant is vast, encompassing two floors, and the service friendly and slick, it packs out quickly. Go early.

Buvette

28 rue Henry Monnier, 9th
Open daily

Yes, it's a little odd to seek out an outpost of a New York interpretation of a French brasserie in Paris, but you should. Against all odds, Buvette is actually very good. They combine an American ethos (all-day dining, attentive service) with carefully sourced French produce, working with celebrated Parisian suppliers including L'Arbe à Café and Terroirs d'Avenir. Start with coffee and pastries in the morning, snack on a croque-monsieur at lunch, or settle in for small plates in the evening. As well as still running their West Village original, they've also opened a restaurant in Tokyo.

Café Marlette

51 rue des Martyrs, 9th
Open daily, daytime only
marlette.fr

Run by two sisters, Marlette began life as an organic start-up selling partially prepared mixes for muffins, madeleines, and crêpes to time-poor but ingredient-conscious Parisians. You can still buy these mixes, as well as granola and gluten-free cake mixes, at their café on rue des Martyrs. It's a rare spot that makes a point of being vegetarian-friendly, and the breakfast and lunch menus are healthy without being too faddy—think open avocado sandwiches and grain bowls. In the afternoon, stop for a coffee with a cookie or piece of carrot cake. No one's judging if you go for a second slice.

Pink Mama

20bis rue de Douai, 9th
Open daily
bigmammagroup.com

Another Big Mama Group creation, this Pigalle outpost is an improbable combination of boxy modern architecture, reflective pink tiling, modern-rustic design, and "like nonna used to make" pasta and pizza. Most dishes are named with their trademark style of humor—from Pesto Pasta Party to Miam Miam (yummy) grilled peppers. Steak is their specialty, so come hungry to share a *fiorentina* (T-bone) or tomahawk (rib steak) with a bowl of cheesy polenta on the side. If you can, check out the rooftop conservatory and the basement speakeasy before leaving. Get here early for your pick of the tables (they don't take reservations).

La REcyclerie

83 boulevard Ornano, 18th
Open daily
larecyclerie.com

Café, restaurant, and urban farm in one, La REcyclerie has transformed an old railway station into warm, welcoming, and light-filled spaces celebrating "eco-responsible" values. What does that mean? An airy cantine with mismatched tables, where you can stop for superb home-cooked food (vegetarian only on Thursdays) or €1 filter coffees. Tables outside by the old railway tracks are ideal for an apéro in summer, and there's a roster of regular events and workshops on everything from mindfulness to how to build your own terrarium. At night expect cocktails and diverse DJ sets—the perfect contrast to a day spent at the nearby Les Puces de Saint-Ouen fleamarket.

Restaurant Belle Maison

4 rue de Navarin, 9th
Closed Sunday and Monday
restaurant-bellemaison.com

Leave the Montmartre crowds behind and walk south for 10 minutes to find this modern bistro. Fish is their focus—think artistically plated swordfish with roasted beetroot and horseradish, or langoustine gyoza—but they reserve around 10 percent of the menu for meatier options, perhaps lamb with dates and smoked yogurt. Whatever you pick, sustainable sourcing is at the heart of their ethos and the fish is line-caught whenever possible. All in all, it's the perfect spot for a romantic meal, although it's wise to make a reservation to be sure of getting a table in the evening.

Roberta

5 rue la Vieuville, 18th
Open daily for lunch and dinner; deli open all day
roberta.fr

Swap the Parisian tradition of apéro for an Italian aperitivo. A mother-and-son team owns Roberta's two restaurants—one here, the other in Bercy, a neighborhood in the southeast of the city. They bring a slice of easygoing Italian charm to the French capital with fresh pasta, imported charcuterie, and gelato from Pozzetto. Their Montmartre trattoria is just around the corner from *Le mur des je t'aime* and offers a welcome breath of fresh air amid the overpriced crêperies that surround the Sacré-Cœur. You could stop by just for a drink and a few plates of prosciutto, or you could settle in for a seasonal feast, perhaps burrata with asparagus pesto followed by trofie (Ligurian pasta twists) with prawns and zucchini. It's an airy space at any time of year, but it's particularly pleasant in spring and summer when they throw open the floor-to-ceiling doors onto the street.

BARS

Les Commères

31 rue Victor Massé, 9th
Closed Sunday and Monday, evenings only

Sweet-toothed travelers, get ready to celebrate. This Pigalle dessert and cocktail bar will cater to your every sugar-based fantasy. Not only can you top your vodka-caramel-coffee cocktail with whipped cream, but you can order a Chantilly-cream stuffed saint-honoré to go with it. Or you could go for a passion fruit and pineapple tart with a Caribbean-inspired rum, ginger beer, and lime punch. There are a few concessions for those with a more savory palate: selections of cured meats, smoked salmon, and grilled vegetables, plus Paris-brewed craft beers from the likes of Deck & Donohue.

Glass

7 rue Frochot, 9th
Daily until 4 a.m.
quixotic-projects.com

A rue Frochot institution, Glass offers one of the few real slices of Americana you're likely to find in Paris. This is no imitation dive bar, but a proper loud and dark late-night spot, where the action gets going around midnight and continues well into the early hours. It's run by Quixotic Projects—the same team behind Candelaria and Les Grands Verres—a group that knows how to make an unexpected theme a roaring success. To drink, there's craft beer, boilermakers, and seriously strong cocktails. Feeling a bit peckish? Order a mustard-laced or pico de gallo–topped hot dog.

Grand Pigalle Hôtel

29 rue Victor Massé, 9th
Open daily
grandpigalle.com

Sinking into a velvet chesterfield at the Grand Pigalle Hôtel bar is just the antidote to a day of sightseeing. While this candle-lit lounge is part of the hotel of the same name, thanks to a series of street-level windows and a separate entrance it feels like a destination in its own right. The classy midnight-blue theme and cocktails around the €15 mark (try the Rum Old Fashioned) also mean it's a touch more grown-up than some of its neighbors. The hotel's chef is Italian, so there's top-quality imported charcuterie and mozzarella to snack on if you get hungry.

Les Justes

1 rue Frochot, 9th
Closed Sunday
lesjustes-pigalle.com

Amid the ever-growing range of cocktail spots on and around rue Frochot, Les Justes continues to stand out as one of the best. It's a warm and relaxed little bar—larger than you'd think from the street—with a laid-back neighborhood feel. It opens earlier than many of the bars nearby, and you'll be just as at home if you come for a sundowner as a 1 a.m. nightcap. Pleasingly, the menu is almost as quirky as the fern-print wallpaper and emerald-blue walls, but they're serious about good mixology. Order an *On Dirait le Sud* (It Looks Like the South) for a delicate blend of olive-infused The Botanist gin, grapefruit liqueur, and lime juice. Prices mostly range from €10 to €15.

Le Vin au Vert

70 rue de Dunkerque, 9th
Closed Sunday and Monday

Sometimes, only a magnum will do. And this caviste-meets-wine bar is just the spot to pick up a party-sized bottle of grower champagne or obscure natural red. They do regular-sized bottles, too, and snacks like burrata and saucisson. They offer a very reasonable corkage fee of around €10 if you just can't wait to open your new discovery. It's a little out of the way, stranded between Pigalle and Gare du Nord, but getting there is well worth a petit diversion.

Le Vrai Paris

33 rue des Abbesses, 18th
Open daily

Beneath its flower-bedecked yellow canopies, Le Vrai Paris might not be an authentic local café—but it's all the more lovely for its obvious play on Montmartre's reputation for romance. Set just off a little square by *Le mur*

LE VRAI PARIS

des je t'aime, it's the ideal apéro spot. It's the kind of place where you can settle in beneath the heaters with a *kir pêche* (white wine with peach liqueur) and a good book, then look up three hours later to realize the stars have come out and a late dinner down the road is beckoning. Their streetfront decorations change with the seasons, moving from boughs of pink blossom in spring to sparser neon illuminations in winter.

SHOPPING

L'Atelier de la Bougie

5 rue des Trois Frères, 18th
Open daily
latelierdelabougie.com

This unusual candle shop doesn't just sell their own scents, but a carefully selected mix of local and international brands. Kerzon candles are all made in France and make great gifts or souvenirs, particularly their line of fragrances named after Parisian landmarks, from Île Saint-Louis (tuberose and jasmine) to Place des Vosges (rose and geranium). Those from Mademoiselle Lulubelle are darker and more sultry, heavy on sandalwood, musk, and spice. Imports include Rewined, whose wine-scented candles hail from Charleston, South Carolina. They also sell a small range of diffusers and home fragrance sprays.

Ferme Saint Hubert

36 rue de Rochechouart, 9th
Closed Sunday

Close your eyes, picture yourself in a little farm shop in rural France, and you might get close to the sensory experience of crossing the threshold of this traditional crèmerie. While you're aware that the center of Paris is steps away, the smell of their 350 cheeses is totally all encompassing: thick slabs of Pont l'Évêque, blue flecked-slices of roquefort, wheels of brie with veins of black truffle, and paper-wrapped hearts of neufchâtel. Opposite the cheese counter, overseen by a herd of porcelain cows, are tins and jars of local and imported specialties ranging from authentic Genoan pesto to gourmet tins of rillettes. And, of course, there's even a small wine selection, heavy on reds that will pair perfectly with your pungent loot. Don't be put off by the shop's slightly out-of-the-way location: You'll be joining plenty of locals popping in to pick up something special for that evening's apéro.

Paperdolls

5 rue Houdon, 18th
Open daily
paperdolls.fr

Paperdolls is as cute as concept stores come. Designed like an apartment rather than a shop, it's a pleasure to browse. It's split into sections showing the wares of 20 handpicked independent designers, mostly small French labels. Their clothing and accessories collections are feminine but not cutesy: think racks of elegant floral dresses, delicate gold jewelry laid out on antique vanities, and recycled stationery displayed on stacks of retro suitcases. Some items are new, others vintage, but all are well priced: perhaps €100 for a silk top or €40 for an unusual ring. "C'est trop cool," as the locals say.

Les Puces de Saint-Ouen

Closest métro: Porte de Clignancourt
Open Saturday, Sunday, and Monday

Paris's premier antiques market is no longer quite the bargain-filled treasure trove it once was—for that you need to head south to the Marché aux Puces de Vanves—but browsing the wares of its 1,000 or so traders is still a must-do experience. Les Puces de Saint-Ouen is actually made up of 14 individual markets, each with its own specialization, from upscale antique furniture to jewels and tableware. Some, like Le Marché Biron, are strictly for serious collectors with cash to spend; in others you'll find beautiful posters, books, and silverware.

Sept Cinq

54 rue Notre-Dame de Lorette, 9th
Closed Sunday and Monday
sept-cinq.com

As international labels crop up more and more in Paris, it's refreshing to find a concept store that specializes in all things Parisian. Created by school friends Audrey and Lorna, Sept Cinq showcases products made by artisans in the city. You never know exactly what you might find there: Collections range from handmade coin purses and tropical-print portable charging packs to silk scarves, red velour boots, and leather sneakers. Their selection of watches is particularly unique—and affordable—kicking off around €80. They have another boutique in the 1st arrondissement near Les Halles.

CHAPTER 6

Canal Saint-Martin to Bastille

L azy afternoons spent along the Canal Saint-Martin are some of the greatest pleasures of visiting Paris. Commissioned in 1802 by Napoleon Bonaparte to create a new supply route into the city, the canal now marks a new center of Paris. This side of the city is where coffee shops first wrestled Parisians from their shots of bitter espresso, where boutiques like Antoine et Lili bought color to a long-neglected part of the city, and where grungy music venues and tiny natural wine bars have led trends around the world.

The canal is over 2.5 miles long, but most of the action is along the mile-long stretch bordered by the quai de Jemmapes and the quai de Valmy. It's crisscrossed by pretty green footbridges, punctuated by working locks, and lined by leafy chestnut trees. In summer, you can barely find space to sit cross-legged on the waterside cobbles as crowds descend with beers and bottles of rosé. This is, of course, also where Amélie famously skimmed her stones in Jean-Pierre Jeunet's kooky comedy.

To the east is the 11th arrondissement. The streets between Oberkampf and Ménilmontant are now some of the city's most-sought after with soaring apartment prices to match. Nowhere else in Paris has such as concentration of great bars and restaurants. You'll find everything from Michelin-starred multicourse tasting menus and innovative small-plate dining to superb Vietnamese bò bún and authentic Neapolitan pizza. Then there are rooftop bars, lovely local cafés, and outstanding pâtisseries. Even if you don't stay nearby, you should certainly come to this area for at least one meal during your trip. At night, things get busy. Rue Jean-Pierre Timbaud and rue Saint-Maur are among the roads lined with small bars whose laid-back terrasses stay open well into the early hours over the weekend.

Amid all the excellent places to eat, there are also some sights to seek out—both modern and historical. Aftter immersing yourself in modern art at the groundbreaking Atelier des Lumières, walk farther south through the 11th and into the 12th arrondissement. There's generally a

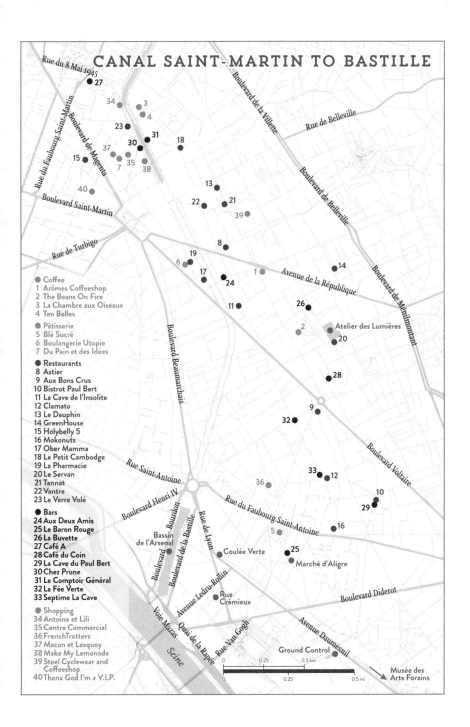

CANAL SAINT-MARTIN TO BASTILLE

Rue du 8 Mai 1945
Boulevard de la Villette
Rue de Belleville
Boulevard de Belleville
Boulevard de Ménilmontant
Rue du Faubourg Saint-Martin
Boulevard de Magenta
Boulevard Saint-Martin
Rue de Turbigo
Avenue de la République
Atelier des Lumières
Boulevard Beaumarchais
Boulevard Voltaire
Rue Saint-Antoine
Boulevard Henri IV
Boulevard Bourdon
Rue de Lyon
Rue de la Bastille
Bassin de l'Arsenal
Rue du Faubourg Saint-Antoine
Boulevard de la Bastille
Coulée Verte
Marché d'Aligre
Avenue Ledru-Rollin
Rue Crémieux
Boulevard Diderot
Voie Mazas
Quai de la Rapée
Rue Van Gogh
Seine
Ground Control
Avenue Daumesnil
Musée des Arts Forains

● Coffee
1 Arômes Coffeeshop
2 The Beans On Fire
3 La Chambre aux Oiseaux
4 Ten Belles

● Pâtisserie
5 Blé Sucré
6 Boulangerie Utopie
7 Du Pain et des Idées

● Restaurants
8 Astier
9 Aux Bons Crus
10 Bistrot Paul Bert
11 La Cave de l'Insolite
12 Clamato
13 Le Dauphin
14 GreenHouse
15 Holybelly 5
16 Mokonuts
17 Ober Mamma
18 Le Petit Cambodge
19 La Pharmacie
20 Le Servan
21 Tannat
22 Vantre
23 Le Verre Volé

● Bars
24 Aux Deux Amis
25 Le Baron Rouge
26 La Buvette
27 Café A
28 Café du Coin
29 La Cave du Paul Bert
30 Chez Prune
31 Le Comptoir Général
32 La Fée Verte
33 Septime La Cave

● Shopping
34 Antoine et Lili
35 Centre Commercial
36 FrenchTrotters
37 Macon et Lesquoy
38 Make My Lemonade
39 Steel Cyclewear and Coffeeshop
40 Thanx God I'm a V.I.P.

0   0.25   0.5 km
0   0.25   0.5 mi

quieter and more residential feel as you approach the Marché d'Aligre. One of the city's largest indoor-outdoor markets, it's been held here since the 1800s and the surrounding streets are jam-packed with fruit, vegetable, and flower stalls every day of the week.

Nearby, sprawling and traffic-choked Place de la Bastille was the site of an infamous prison until the 1789 revolution. Today it's distinguished by the modern Opéra Bastille on its eastern side and the 52-meter-high Colonne de Juillet at its center. Venture away from the main roads to the south and you might be surprised to stumble onto the candy-colored rue Crémieux and the Bassin de l'Arsenal, a pretty working port that could have been transported straight from the south of France. It's a lovely spot for a peaceful walk, as is the Coulée Verte—an old railway line converted into an elevated walkway—that starts just a short stroll away.

A little farther east, those in search of the unusual shouldn't miss the astonishing Musée des Arts Forains, dedicated to the world of fairground arts; and the cool arts space and street food venue, Ground Control.

SEE

Atelier des Lumières

38 rue Saint-Maur, 11th
Open daily
atelier-lumieres.com

You'll find "the world's first digital art museum" on a quiet backstreet deep in the 11th arrondissement. Taking over an old iron foundry, it displays artworks like you've never seen them before—as part of an immersive audio and visual 360-degree experience created by more than 100 projectors designed to bring great masters to a new audience. Gustav Klimt and Hundertwasser were among the first artists to get the Lumières treatment, Klimt's glittering *The Kiss* transformed into a 10-meter-high shimmering marvel. Each show runs for several months, and you'll need to buy timed tickets in advance online to be sure to get in during your desired slot.

CLOCKWISE FROM TOP LEFT: MORNING ALONG THE CANAL SAINT-MARTIN; GRAFFITI IN THE 11TH ARRONDISSEMENT; RUE CREMIEUX

Marché d'Aligre

Place d'Aligre, 12th

Tuesday to Sunday mornings; indoor market also open in the afternoons

If you only have time to visit one food market, make it the Marché d'Aligre. Six days a week vendors cram into streets surrounding the small covered market building on Place d'Aligre, the roads entirely blocked by stalls laden with fresh produce. In the covered market itself you'll find superb cheese shops and butchers, and there are myriad specialty independent stores in the roads nearby. At weekends, bric-a-brac sellers and florists often join the mix. Shopping here is busy, loud, and overwhelming—and you might find you want to do a lap before you enter into negotiations over the best *fraises* (strawberries) for your picnic or stop to inspect fresh herbs. You'll find the pick of the produce early in the morning when the market is at its most energetic. Come noon, do as the locals do and retire to Le Baron Rouge for a glass of wine or stop for lunch at one of the many excellent cafés and restaurants that thrive on the market's edges.

Rue Crémieux

12th

Rue Crémieux's candy-colored houses have become an internet sensation—H&M even named a blush-pink perfume in their honor—somewhat to the chagrin of residents who've been reduced to putting notices in their windows, such as "please do not photograph my cat." Still, these sweet cottage-style row houses, built in the mid-1800s and now decorated with wall paintings of flowering vines and fronted by lush window boxes, are well worth coming to see. Just be respectful and remember it's a residential neighborhood not a photo-shoot backdrop. The street is close to the start of the Promenade Plantée, so it's easy to incorporate a visit into a longer stroll; a few minutes is plenty to admire the architecture and snap a (discreet) photo.

BASSIN DE L'ARSENAL

Bassin de l'Arsenal

Boulevard de la Bastille, 12th

Efforts are being made to make the Bassin de l'Arsenal more accessible from Place de la Bastille, but it will always feel a world away from Paris. This little tree-lined port was built as a commercial harbor in the early 1800s, and it now provides moorings to 200 or so vessels, ranging from live-aboard houseboats to private pleasure boats. Few know that you can actually hop aboard Seine cruises here, or start a journey upstream on sightseeing trips along the Canal Saint-Martin toward the Bassin de la Villette. On the eastern bank there's a small but pretty garden, fragranced by rose bushes and clematis in summer, and a simple café-bar with plenty of outdoor tables.

Coulée Verte

Avenue Daumesnil, 12th

The delightful Coulée Verte (also known as the Promenade Plantée) opened back in 1988, transforming an abandoned railway line into a tranquil footpath running more than 2 miles out of the city to the Bois de Vincennes. You might think it's Paris's answer to the High Line—but it was actually the inspiration for New York's landmark redevelopment. The route is lined with tiny rose gardens, fragrant lavender bushes, and vine-draped archways. It's one of the best spots to see the first spring blossoms, or to go for a bracing walk away from the city traffic in winter. The path is hidden from the streets below and is only connected to ground level by elevator and stairs at certain points: the first entrance on avenue Daumesnil, just where it splits from rue de Lyon, is the easiest place to start.

Ground Control

81 rue du Charolais, 12th
Closed Monday and Tuesday
groundcontrolparis.com

Ground Control, one of the coolest concept spaces to open in Paris in the last few years, took over the Halle Charolais, a simply enormous warehouse on the edge of the Gare de Lyon. Ascend a metal staircase and you enter a huge terrace where street food traders occupy the shells of reconditioned buses and métro carriages, and locals pack the tables on sunny days. Inside, the vibe is community center–meets–house party, with several distinct spaces. The main event is the halle à manger, where lines of 30-person-long benches are surrounded, food-court style, by excellent food options that include Argentine, Mexican, and Chinese cuisine, and a handful of bars. Elsewhere you'll find table tennis, arcade games, galleries, pop-up shops, the shell of a passenger jet (complete with original seats), and open spaces used for everything from talks to yoga classes.

Musée des Arts Forains

53 avenue des Terroirs de France, 12th
Prebooked tours usually run three days a week; other events and festivals run
throughout the year.
arts-forains.com

There aren't many museums where you can take a spin on a fairground carousel from the early 1900s—but at the Musée des Arts Forains you can. This totally one-of-a-kind museum offers an over-the-top introduction to the art of the Belle Époque funfair. Inside four sprawling warehouses far to the southeast of Bastille—once used by traders bringing wines from Bordeaux into the city—you're transported back in time to an era of beautiful carousels, garish fairground games, and riotous carnivals. But the exhibits are not just here to look at: You get a chance to try a handful of them for yourself. Tours kick off in song, perhaps as you perch awkwardly on an ornate carved swan, and include sound-and-light shows, animatronics, and a ride on a carousel in each of the enormous pavilions. If you're lucky, and brave, you might even get to hop aboard a bike on a pedal-powered manège invented in England in the 1800s—although reaching speeds of around 30 mph with nothing in the way of safety measures is not for the fainthearted.

COFFEE

Arômes Coffeeshop

86 avenue Parmentier, 11th
Open daily

The big appeal at this coffee bar is the swinging basket chairs in the window, where you can sip the perfect flat white and watch life go by on busy avenue Parmentier. Service is relaxed and unhurried, and you might spot some great latte art at quieter moments. Stay resolutely Parisian with a *café noisette* (espresso lengthened with a little hot milk) or warm up with one of the best ranges of hot chocolates in the city. In the morning, sugar-dusted and fruit-topped waffles (as well as seasonal specials like chestnut purée) are offered, and at lunch savory options and salads.

The Beans on Fire

7 rue du Général Blaise, 11th
Open daily
thebeansonfire.com

The Beans on Fire stands out among the 11ème's coffee shops for several reasons. First, they're a leader in their field. They roast their own beans on-site and they also offer "collaborative roasting," meaning they let others use their facilities and run workshops on the craft. The other big attraction is their outdoor tables on peaceful Square Maurice Gardette, a lovely spot for a sunny morning espresso or a milky latte in winter. Their food menu isn't extensive, but there are usually cakes, cookies, and the like on offer.

La Chambre aux Oiseaux

48 rue Bichat, 10th
Open daily

Parisian coffee shops are often cool but rarely cozy. La Chambre aux Oiseaux is one of the few to buck the trend with its scuffed wooden tables, squidgy armchairs, and floral wallpaper—and it's only steps from the Canal Saint-Martin. Even if you intend to just stop by for a latte, you're unlikely to be able to resist the homemade cakes and muffins, prettily displayed on the counter in domed glass cake stands. At lunch the menu widens to include things like simple goat's cheese salads and seasonal soups. For breakfast they offer toast and jam, and weekends feature a more extensive savory brunch menu.

Ten Belles

10 rue de la Grange aux Belles, 10th
Open daily

This minimalist, pint-sized coffee shop was one of the early drivers of the transformation of the Canal Saint-Martin and remains one of the biggest names on the Parisian specialty coffee scene. There might not be many seats, but their coffees are superb, whether ordered to go or to drink in. Cookies and banana bread will sate your hunger here, but head south to their bakery, Ten Belles Bread (17–19 rue Breguet, 11th), and you'll find everything from focaccia sandwiches and pulled-pork buns to meringue-topped tarts—although the setting is a little less atmospheric.

PÂTISSERIE

Blé Sucré

7 rue Antoine Vollon, 12th
Closed Monday; Sunday, morning only

Some bakeries are so good they get by without websites and Instagram accounts, drawing in customers on their word-of-mouth reputation alone. That's not to say Blé Sucré hasn't had plenty of press: This boulangerie and pâtisserie on Square Armand Trousseau counts awards for the best baguettes in Paris and rave reviews from the *New York Times* among its accolades. Perhaps this is no surprise, given that Blé Sucré was founded (though is no longer run) by Fabrice Le Bourdat, who previously worked on the pastry team at Le Bristol, one of the grandes dames of the five-star hotel scene. What should you order? Lemony madeleines or their unusually airy yet rich croissants are the perfect options to eat as you wander the nearby Marché d'Aligre.

Boulangerie Utopie

20 rue Jean-Pierre Timbaud, 11th
Closed Monday

While Du Pain et des Idées has been discovered by visitors and magazines the world over, nearby Boulangerie Utopie remains more of a local secret. It might look small and simple, but the line running out the door every morning attests that their baking is anything but. Baguettes, pains au chocolat, and croissants are their mainstay, but the desserts are something *really* special. Highlights include glossy pistachio tarts, Japanese-inspired black sesame éclairs, and cakes that might blend flavors such as coriander and mango. Be sure to check out their Instagram, where they religiously showcase new creations each week. Service is always with a smile, and you're likely to get a nod of recognition if you visit more than once.

Du Pain et des Idées

34 rue Yves Toudic, 10th
Closed Saturday and Sunday
dupainetdesidees.com

If you've seen one pastry in photos before you get to Paris, it's likely to have been Du Pain et des Idées's famous escargot chocolat-pistache. Yet as delicious as these flaky chocolate and pistachio scrolls are, they're not the bakery's focus. Du Pain et des Idées was started by Christophe Vasseur, who quit a career in fashion to revive centuries-old bread-making traditions in this historic bakery (dating back to the late 1800s). His breads and baguettes are made with sourdough starters and little yeast, differing from many others in Paris. The most celebrated loaf is his pain des amis, which is deeply flavored with a dark crust. The pains au chocolat (controversially called chocolatines, a name hailing from the south of France) are also superb.

CLOCKWISE FROM THE TOP: BOULANGERIE UTOPIE; TEN BELLES BREAD; ARÔMES COFFEESHOP

RESTAURANTS

Astier

44 rue Jean-Pierre Timbaud, 11th
Daily lunch and dinner
restaurant-astier.com

This old-fashioned bistro is exactly the kind of place you'd want in your hometown. With no fancy façade or pavement tables, Astier is short on curb appeal in some regards but more than compensates with its crowd-pleasing menu. Although ownership has changed over the years, they've held much the same ethos since they opened in 1956: quality French produce classically cooked. Hearty dishes like roasted duck breast or bouillabaisse (around €30) might be the main event, but save room for something sweet. Desserts are a big deal here: You can't go wrong with a *baba au rhum* (a yeasted doughnut drenched in rum at your table), or their Grand Marnier soufflé, designed to share.

Aux Bons Crus

54 rue Godefroy Cavaignac, 11th
Open daily, lunch only on Sunday
auxbonscrus.fr

Aux Bons Crus brings to life France's rather more chic equivalent of the roadside diner—specifically gourmet but affordable restaurants recommended by institution Les Routiers, whose sign is proudly displayed outside. Reinvented for discerning Parisian dinners rather than long-haul truck drivers, they specialize in dishes with a Lyonnaise twist, all served on gingham tablecloths and washed down with little pichets of wine. Try their céleri rémoulade with crab to start, then tuck into *quenelles de brochet* (creamed fish dumplings, a Lyonnaise specialty) or *rognons de veau à la Dijonnaise* (veal kidneys in a mustardy sauce). It's fresh, classic cooking done well—and there's calvados granita for dessert. *Plats* start at just €15.

Bistrot Paul Bert

18 rue Paul Bert, 11th

Closed Sunday and Monday, lunch and dinner

Bistrot Paul Bert is no secret—this delightfully old-school restaurant has been *the* place to order steak-frites for years—but its quality and style never diminishes. It offers everything you could want from a classic Parisian bistro: mottled antique mirrors, tiled walls, red-leather chairs, and a chalkboard menu of French classics. A set three-course meal is usually around €40. Start with buttery scallops served in the half shell, stay traditional with tartare or steak for the main event, and finish with their famous Paris-Brest, a wheel-shaped choux pastry filled with praline cream invented to celebrate the 1910 Paris to Brest cycle race.

La Cave de L'Insolite

30 rue de la Folie Méricourt, 11th

Closed Monday

This neighborhood wine bar and restaurant is a relaxed spot for dinner. Thanks to an eclectic mix of spindle-backed chairs, bar seats, and sharing tables, you'll be just as welcome for a glass of wine as a meal. The menu is also pleasingly inventive. Instead of wine-bar-staple cheese and charcuterie platters, you might find seared tuna in a peach and apricot soup or *bavette* (flank steak) with grenaille potatoes. Plats are around €25. Finish your meal with a crème caramel or a sophisticated interpretation of an After Eight, incorporating chocolate mousse and mint ice cream.

Clamato

80 rue de Charonne, 11th
Closed Monday and Tuesday
clamato-charonne.fr

Quirky-cool seafood restaurant Clamato has made a big splash. Behind the plain sea-green facade is a no-frills dining room where all the focus is on the food. If you're unsure whether to opt for huîtres plates or huîtres creuses, staff are clued-up and happy to dole out tips in English. The menu changes daily but might include dishes like pollack croquettes, scallops with herb butter, black mullet ceviche, or rock crab with dill mayo. Just don't turn up expecting to eat immediately: Their no reservations policy means you may need to find a nearby bar for a few drinks before they call to say your table is ready. It's owned by the same team behind Septime and Septime La Cave.

Le Dauphin

131 avenue Parmentier, 11th
Closed Sunday and Monday
restaurantledauphin.net

Marble-topped bar tables and mirrored walls set the tone at Le Dauphin. In the evenings they claim to serve tapas, but what's really on offer is a selection of affordable small plates that are more French than Spanish in style. The menu changes daily, so you could find yourself plunging artichoke petals into anchovy-spiked mayonnaise, scooping up creamy spoonfuls of burrata topped with trout roe, or savoring slices of rare pigeon breast. By contrast their lunch menu has more of an Asian twist: Spicy noodle soups are the main event. If budget is no concern, sister restaurant Le Chateaubriand next door offers a no-choice tasting menu for €75.

CLOCKWISE FROM TOP LEFT: LA CAVE DE L'INSOLITE; CLAMATO; MOKOUNUTS; LE SERVAN

GreenHouse

22 rue Crespin du Gast, 11th
Closed Sunday and Monday

At Kristin Frederick's natural wine bar and restaurant, the menu is anything but traditional. To accompany an unusual pét-nat or quirky red, you can order crispy-bottomed gyoza or even KFC—that's Kentucky-fried *chou fleur* (cauliflower) for the uninitiated. But the real highlights on the menu are the tacos. Pull up a bar seat and prepare to get messy tucking into slow-cooked beef and guacamole or tempura veg. Expect to spend around €45 on food and drinks to leave full and very content.

Holybelly 5

5 rue Lucien Sampaix, 10th
Open daily
holybellycafe.com

The concept of brunch has taken Paris by storm. And if you get a craving for pancakes, there's simply nowhere better than Holybelly. This is their second no-reservations outpost, opened after demand for their legendary short stacks outstripped the kitchen's abilities at their first restaurant up the road. Expats and locals alike rave about their decidedly un-French menu, which has brought chia pudding, hash browns, and cornbread to a new and rapturous audience. The other secret to their success is superb service: always friendly, attentive, and welcoming.

Mokonuts

5 rue Saint-Bernard, 11th
Monday to Friday breakfast and lunch only

Run by the ever-friendly Moko and Omar—whose backgrounds span Lebanon, Japan, London, and San Francisco—this teeny white-walled café is a firm favorite among food-loving locals. From its miniscule kitchen come magical creations: perhaps an heirloom zucchini salad beautifully arranged on a dove-gray bowl, homemade bread to dunk into creamy labneh topped with za'atar, or crispy-skinned chicken breasts with fresh vegetables and potatoes. Above all, they're famed for their cookies: served warm and studded with molten chocolate chunks or coated in sesame seeds. It's only open during the day: Expect to spend around €30, more if you order a bottle of (natural) wine.

Ober Mama

107 boulevard Richard Lenoir, 11th
Daily lunch and dinner
bigmammagroup.com

If you like the sound of a build-your-own negroni menu, wood-fired pizzas, and antipasti plates laden with mortadella, salami, and coppa, then Big Mamma's sprawling Oberkampf outpost is your temple. They might even be solely responsible for Parisians' serious Aperol obsession. Portions are enormous, staff are almost entirely Italian, and diners are young and loud. That's not to say they don't take the food seriously. If you've got money to spend then you won't be lacking in options, from bottles of Franciacorta, Italy's answer to champagne, to fresh-truffle pasta. Better still is their list of sparkling red wines; Lambrusco is finally back in fashion.

Le Petit Cambodge

20 rue Alibert, 10th
Open daily
lepetitcambodge.fr

This isn't the most authentic spot in Paris for Southeast Asian food, but it is one of the most fun with its bright yellow awnings and rainbow-colored metal chairs. Bò bún is the big attraction. Not actually a Cambodian dish, as you might expect from restaurant's name, but a Vietnamese one, bò bún is a hot-and-cold mix of rice noodles topped with herbs, vegetables, peanuts, and usually beef or prawns. They do plenty of vegetarian options, too, as well as soups, curries, and summer rolls. There's a second branch on the other side of the canal on rue Beaurepaire.

CLOCKWISE FROM TOP LEFT: LE DAUPHIN; TANNAT; OBER MAMA

La Pharmacie

22 rue Jean-Pierre Timbaud, 11th
Open daily lunch and dinner
restaurant-lapharmacie.fr

This restaurant hides behind a picturesque teal-blue façade of a former pharmacy. It's a warm and welcoming one-service-a-night kind of place on the quieter end of rue Jean-Pierre Timbaud, where good cooking and quality ingredients trump the latest fad. Classic techniques don't mean a boring menu, though: plats (around €20) might include cod with black-garlic cream or milk-fed lamb with turnip purée. There's usually at least one vegetarian option, too. Desserts, usually including a tarte tatin and *mi-cuit chocolat noir* (melting-middle dark chocolate cake), are worth sticking around for.

Le Servan

32 rue Saint-Maur, 11th
Closed Saturday and Sunday

The word neo-bistro gets bandied around a lot, but Le Servan is one of the few places to have really played a part in the transformation of the city's dining scene. Sisters Tatiana and Katia made their reputation for bold ingredient-led cooking, serving *tête de veau* (veal head) and *boudin noir* wontons (made with blood sausage) in their modern, light-filled restaurant. Less adventurous pairings are no less impressive, many with an Asian twist, such as cod with a pistachio-lime sauce, or pork with grilled eggplant and fried tofu. In short, the food is simply superb and an excellent value with plats usually below €30. If you want a culinary adventure without a white tablecloth in sight, this is the place to come. The gold-topped bar is also great spot for solo dining.

Tannat

119 avenue Parmentier, 11th
Closed Sunday
tannat.fr

This grown-up, brick-walled bistro hits just the right spot between refined and exciting. Those in the know come for their excellent-value set menus, starting from around €15 for two courses at lunch time during the week. With big picture windows, it's a buzzy spot to eat during the day. Dishes are light, seasonal, and colorful—and always beautifully plated. White asparagus might be paired with quail eggs and elderberries, or you could find a lamb dish scattered with cocoa nibs. Like the sound of a chocolate-sage mousse or a baba with hibiscus, kiwi, and passion fruit? Don't skip dessert, where classical techniques meet unconventional flavors.

Vantre

19 rue de la Fontaine au Roi, 11th
Closed Saturday and Sunday
vantre.fr

Don't be fooled into thinking Vantre is just a local spot. Its casual appearance is deceiving: Some serious cooking goes into their *cuisine du marché* (market cooking). They also have one of the city's most extensive wine lists—and can offer plenty of advice on pairings, particularly for the cheese plate you must order if you have room before dessert. The rest of the menu is firmly rooted in tradition, with combinations like sage butter gnocchi and lamb with artichokes. A single plat is around €30, or you can get settled in for multicourse tasting menus in the evening.

Le Verre Volé

67 rue de Lancry, 10th
Daily lunch and dinner
leverrevole.fr

With its mismatched tables and bottle-lined walls, Le Verre Volé is the quintessential no-frills canalside hangout. It's also somewhat a place of pilgrimage for natural wine devotees. These days, they have an English menu and plenty of curious visitors, but the food is no less exciting. Wine, of course, is the big attraction. There's no list, so you'll need to be prepared to follow recommendations. Expect to pay around €30–40 for a memorable bottle, perhaps Laurent Cazottes' Adèle, a gorgeous white made from the rare grape Mauzac Rosé. Dishes of the day could range from ceviche to *boudin noir* (blood sausage), with classics like chocolate mousse to finish.

BARS

Aux Deux Amis

45 rue Oberkampf, 11th
Closed Sunday and Monday

This bare-bones spot in Oberkampf was one of the city's first big natural wine bars—and it's still one of the coolest places for an apéro. Come early to bag one of the coveted seats at the copper bar, where you can watch plate after plate of charcuterie being sliced while you ogle what everyone else is ordering. Adventurous eaters are rewarded with plates of tartare, terrines, and cheese alongside delicate squid, duck, and mackerel dishes. Late at night it's usually crammed with regulars and industry types. Get your best French ready and try to blend in if you want to squeeze around a Formica table for a nightcap.

If you're eating and drinking in Paris, one thing will appear on nearly every menu: natural wines. You'll soon spot the telltale signs, from quirky labels to their wax-sealed corks. Once poured, they might be slightly cloudy or fizzy, and even if you recognize the grape, the wine may taste quite unlike anything you've drunk before.

So what's the deal with natural wine? Over the past 10 years, there's been a revolution in the winemaking community, driven by a desire to make wines with minimal intervention. That means less sulfur, less chemical or machine processes, and frequently organic and biodynamic viticulture. Often this goes hand-in-hand with small-scale production and the revival of little known and forgotten varieties. The hype around Parisian *bars à vins* is just the start of it. Some producers, such as those in France's Jura region, have ascended to almost rock star status.

The only problem is that there's no official and tangible definition of what constitutes a natural wine. And to say that some of the bolder wines have caused controversy among experts would be an understatement. So how should you approach natural wine? Simply drink, experiment, and enjoy. Here are three styles to look out for:

Chilled red wines: Natural wines are known for breaking the rules. That means you'll find lots of light and fresh reds that are closer to a rosé in color than a plummy Cabernet. They're best drunk chilled, so don't be surprised if you order a glass of Pinot Noir and it comes straight from the cooler.

"Orange" wines: White wines are generally made with grapes that are quickly pressed so that the skins have little to no contact with the juice. Orange or skin-contact wines buck this trend, leaving the skins to macerate with the juice in a process usually reserved for red wines. Not only does this impart color but a whole bunch of exciting new flavors, from floral notes to spicy depths.

Pét-nats: Fizzy pét-nat, or *pétillant naturel* wines to use their proper name, are the cool kids on the sparkling wine block. Unlike champagne, they only undergo one fermentation in the bottle and are often sealed with a metal beer cap. You'll find they have a gentler fizz and may often be slightly cloudy. Some are lower in alcohol, so they're the perfect choice to sip at *apéro* hour.

Le Baron Rouge

1 rue Théophile Roussel, 12th
Open daily, times vary

You can't come to the Marché d'Aligre without stopping for a little glass of wine—drunk standing up at a repurposed barrel table—at this wonderfully old-fashioned bar. While the market's in full swing it's usually quiet, and you can linger over a plate of oysters, cheese, or charcuterie. As soon as the stalls shut down, traders pour in and you'll be jostling for space. The bar features an astonishing 30 or so wines by the glass at any one time, all served in tiny pours from just €3 a pop.

La Buvette

67 rue Saint-Maur, 11th
Closed Monday and Tuesday

Size certainly doesn't matter at La Buvette. Camille Fourmont's laid-back bar might be tiny, but it's one of the most celebrated spots in the city to drink natural wine. Squeeze onto a spare table and ask for her recommendations: perhaps a skin-contact white or unusual Cabernet Franc from the Loire region. There are usually options like charcuterie, terrines, cheeses, and plates of her signature white beans to snack on. It's the perfect spot to stop by for an early glass before heading to a nearby restaurant for dinner. Just note that it's often a one-woman show, so opening hours listed online aren't always that reliable.

Café A

148 rue du Faubourg Saint-Martin, 10th
Open daily until 2 a.m.
cafea.fr

From the outside, Café A doesn't look promising. It's set in an old convent just by Gare de l'Est, concealed by a 3-meter-high metal fence. From the street there's little sign that anything of interest lies inside. Yet slip through the narrow gate and walk along the cloister on the right-hand side and you'll find that the convent's ancient chapel has been transformed into a café, bar, and restaurant that's anything but traditional. Inside, the space has been stripped of all decoration and filled with high bar tables. It's open all day, but it's most fun at night when there are DJs and buckets of iced beers. Outside is a courtyard garden, lit by a forest of fairy lights on warm summer evenings.

Café du Coin

9 rue Camille Desmoulins, 11th
Closed Sunday

This slightly scruffy and delightfully laid-back bar is still pleasingly off the radar of most visitors to Paris. It's the kind of place that prioritizes the food and drink before the "concept" (and painting the walls). By day it's a light-filled restaurant with a much-hyped weekday set menu for around €20 at lunch, and in the evening it transforms into a low-key bar. After 6 p.m., expect natural wine, cocktails, and snacks—generally pizzette, charcuterie, and cheese. You'll quickly feel right at home.

La Cave du Paul Bert

16 rue Paul Bert, 11th
Daily from noon

La Cave Paul Bert couldn't be more different from the eponymous bistro a few doors along. While the restaurant celebrates France's culinary classics in an uber-traditional setting, this tiny no-frills bar champions its winemaking pioneers. There are barely 10 seats inside—most along the counter—with a few more on the street in summer. Their wines by the glass change regularly, so you could drink steely Riesling from Alsace or some unusual fizz from Savoie. Unusually, it's also open from lunchtime through to around midnight every day, making it the perfect spot for a quick verre early in the evening when few wine bars are open.

Chez Prune

36 rue Beaurepaire, 10th
Open daily

This simple café-bar has no obvious draw—no unusual menu, no quirky decor—but night after night it's the first spot to be packed full, with loiterers waiting by the door for tables en terrasse to open up. If you had to define its aesthetic, you could call it shabby chic, but really it's an easy place for a coffee, a glass of wine, or even one last drink on your way home at 2 a.m. Grab a table outdoors if you're in the mood for people watching, or settle in to the mosaic-tiled interior with a book.

Le Comptoir Général

80 quai de Jemmapes, 10th
Open daily
lecomptoirgeneral.com

Nowhere else has generated hype along the Canal Saint-Martin quite like Le Comptoir Général. Is it a ramshackle bar, an art gallery, a greenhouse, or a coworking space? No one quite knows. It's certainly eclectic, mixing

CLOCKWISE FROM TOP LEFT: LA BUVETTE; LE BARON ROUGE; BISTROT PAUL BERT; SEPTIME LA CAVE

influences from across Africa with kitschy vintage furniture. To be honest, it's best not to try to define the vibe too carefully. Just get there early to beat the long lines and then settle in to the early hours with pitchers of potent rum punch. Different bars have different menus, so explore the various rooms before you settle on one spot.

La Fée Verte

108 rue de la Roquette, 11th
Open daily

Artists may no longer cluster in Montmartre for absinthe-fueled evenings, but you can still find the green fairy, elsewhere in Paris. At first glance the nod to absinthe seems to appear only in this corner bar's name—but in addition to serving the usual bistro burgers and pints, they also serve absinthe the proper way: first, you are given a sugar cube to set on a slotted "absinthe spoon" above your glass full of neat spirit; then, you slowly drip distilled water onto the sugar cube from an "absinthe fountain" (a traditional glass tabletop pitcher with taps) until the sugar dissolves and the spirit clouds. Just to get one thing straight, despite all the myths, absinthe today is neither illegal nor a hallucinogen, although it is often upward of 80 proof.

Septime La Cave

3 rue Basfroi, 11th
Daily from 4 p.m.

Getting a reservation at the much-hyped and Michelin-starred neo-bistro Septime is nigh impossible. It's a different story at their cute-as-a-button natural wine bar round the corner. As you'd expect, bottles are meticulously selected. The joy of drinking here isn't to try a wine you've heard about or drunk before, but to taste one you never knew even existed. Floral orange wines are just the start of what could be on offer. If you fall in love with a new winemaker, you can also buy bottles to take away. Sometimes they request that you get a snack with your drink; they serve little plates of olives, saucisson, lardons, and rillettes but nothing more substantial.

SHOPPING

Antoine et Lili

95 quai de Valmy, 10th
Open daily
antoineetlili.com

You can't miss Antoine et Lili's dusky-pink, lime-green, and sunshine-yellow storefronts. They have become landmarks on the banks of the Canal Saint-Martin. This three-part concept store opened here in 1998, its interconnected shops selling bohemian toys, women's wear, and quirky home decorations in turn. You never quite know what you might find: hand-embroidered Mexican cushions, Frida Kahlo notebooks, or Indian-inspired jewelry. There are plenty of souvenir-sized curios, too, from decorative mugs to quirky key chains. They have a strong aesthetic, their eclectic collections tied together by their trademark bright, vivid colors rather than the latest trends.

Centre Commercial

2 rue de Marseille, 10th
Open daily

The men's wear and women's wear collections selected by Sébastien Kopp and François-Ghislain Morillion, founders of sneaker brand Veja, are every bit as good as you'd expect. A commitment to ethical fashion underpins all the brands they showcase, from Church's shoes, made in the United Kingdom, to Grenoble-based Paraboot. You'll also spot better-known names as diverse as Saint James, Birkenstock, and Commes des Garçons, as well as the Veja range, of course. You could easily spend upward of €1,000 on a few items, but you could also find that *perfect* button-down shirt you've been searching for at around €100.

FrenchTrotters

30 rue de Charonne, 11th
Closed Sunday and Monday
frenchtrotters.fr

An original lifestyle store created by Carole and Clarent Dehlouz, FrenchTrotters brings together labels from United States, the Netherlands, France, and elsewhere—as well as selling their own line. Among their men's wear, women's wear, accessories, and home collections you'll also spot plenty of exclusives: pouches made in collaboration with Japanese brand Delfonics, one-off boot designs from Parisian leather goods purveyor Anthology, or unusual wool scarves from Moismont. It's not particularly cheap to shop here, with shirts from €100 and knitwear from €150, but their pieces are impeccably chosen and modern classics; you'll keep them in your wardrobe for years.

Macon et Lesquoy

37 rue Yves Toudic, 10th
Closed Sunday
maconetlesquoy.com

Little mementos and gifts from Paris don't get more unique than Macon et Lesquoy's hand-embroidered badges, patches, and jewelry. Many of their quirky designs humorously play on French clichés, with iron-on slogans like *mon amour!* (my love) and *bise* (kiss). Their beaded pins and brooches are beautiful but understated, ranging from the touristy (Eiffel Towers and Camemberts) to seahorses, lobsters, and shooting stars. None are conventional, and while many of these items are sold in the likes of Galeries Lafayette, only in their boutique can you can see the full selection. The simplest designs start at €10; expect to pay upward of €50 for the most intricate.

Make My Lemonade

61 quai de Valmy, 10th
Closed Monday
makemylemonade.com

The first solo bricks and mortar venture by designer and blogger Lisa Gachet, Make My Lemonade is one of the most original shops along the canal. At the front it's a pastel-hued women's wear boutique, with a small but distinctive collection of casual dungarees, sweatshirts, dresses, and the like depending on the season. At the back you can pick up Gachet's "DIY couture" patterns and bolts of bold, printed fabrics to make everything from shirts to pajamas at home. Hidden even farther back is a secret café, where you can sip a cappuccino topped with edible flowers on a pink velour bench.

Steel Cyclewear & Coffeeshop

58 rue de la Fontaine au Roi, 11th
Closed Sunday and Monday
steelcyclewear.com

Even Lycra is more chic in Paris. Part minimalist coffee shop, part concept cycle store, Steel is one of a kind. You can sip an espresso or a beer while you browse their latest stock, which ranges from the latest shoes and shorts to gloves, helmets, and water bottles, although at the moment, their men's wear collections are more extensive. Staff are super enthusiastic and clued-up, ready to offer advice and share stories whether you're a city cyclist of an off-road enthusiast. Up for a 35-mile ride? Ask them about their weekend Cycle Club, which runs every other weekend.

Thanx God I'm a V.I.P.

12 rue de Lancry, 10th
Closed Sunday
thanxgod.com

Whether you're looking for Margiela and Givenchy or Hermès and Lanvin, check out this impeccably organized vintage store. Color-coordinated racks of high-end men's wear and women's wear are the focus, but you might spot great accessories as well, perhaps a Dior purse or even some Chanel jewelry if you get lucky. All items are a fraction of what they would have cost new, and if you go wild and don't have room in your suitcase for your designer haul, they'll send it back home for you.

CHAPTER 7

Belleville and La Villette

East from the Canal Saint-Martin, the districts become more diverse. Elegant 19th-century apartment blocks become interspersed with postwar high rises as you climb the hill toward Belleville. This was once a village beyond the city limits, but today it's very much in the heart of Paris and is home to numerous immigrant communities, including those from Tunisia, Algeria, and Vietnam. There's a little bit of a culture clash in places, such as around graffiti-clad rue Denoyez where new cafés have moved in to sell €5-a-pop coffees next to halal butcheries and Chinese supermarkets. But mostly it's a fascinating part of Paris to explore—and one that actually reflects the city's cosmopolitan population.

The restaurants alone are reason enough to come here. New spots seem to open each week, and they are supplemented by a rotating roster of traders at the monthly street food market on boulevard Belleville. Whether you're after authentic pho or French small plates cooked by a Brit, you'll find it in this neighborhood. As night falls, the quartier's once grungy but now increasingly cool bars are ideal for starting a night out with great cocktails, and then dancing at club-meet-event spaces like La Bellevilloise. Belleville is also a great place to look for affordable places to stay, particularly by way of design-led apartments and Airbnbs.

Steeply sloping Parc de Belleville marks the center of the neighborhood. It's not particularly leafy, but there are great city vistas across to the Eiffel Tower from its highest point. Beyond, little glimpses of Belleville's village-y side remain around Jourdain métro. If you're in search of green space, the glorious Parc des Buttes-Chaumont is not only one of the highlights of the 19th arrondissement, but perhaps the most magnificent park in Paris. Despite the fact that it encompasses waterfalls, follies, and sprawling lawns—and offers views across to the Sacré-Cœur—it's rarely discovered by first-time visitors to the city. To the south is Père Lachaise, the city's largest and most famous cemetery.

North of Belleville, the Canal de l'Ourcq runs a straight course out to the edges of Paris, starting in the wide Bassin de la Villette, lined with floating bars and locals playing pétanque in good weather. Just inside the

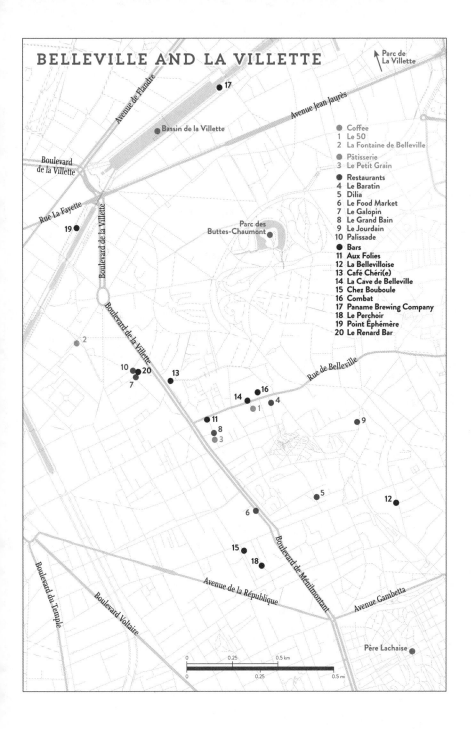

BELLEVILLE AND LA VILLETTE

Parc de
La Villette

Avenue de Flandre

Avenue Jean Jaurès

17

Bassin de la Villette

Boulevard
de la Villette

Rue La Fayette

Boulevard de la Villette

19

Parc des
Buttes-Chaumont

Boulevard de la Villette

● Coffee
1 Le 50
2 La Fontaine de Belleville

● Pâtisserie
3 Le Petit Grain

● Restaurants
4 Le Baratin
5 Dilia
6 Le Food Market
7 Le Galopin
8 Le Grand Bain
9 Le Jourdain
10 Palissade

● Bars
11 Aux Folies
12 La Bellevilloise
13 Café Chéri(e)
14 La Cave de Belleville
15 Chez Bouboule
16 Combat
17 Paname Brewing Company
18 Le Perchoir
19 Point Éphémère
20 Le Renard Bar

2

10 20
7 **13**

Rue de Belleville

14 **16**
1 **4**

11
8
3

9

5

12

6

15
18

Boulevard de Ménilmontant

Boulevard du Temple

Boulevard Voltaire

Avenue de la République

Avenue Gambetta

Père Lachaise

0   0.25   0.5 km

0   0.25   0.5 mi

périphérique it flows into the Parc de la Villette. Once the site of the city's abattoirs, today it's a cultural hub that is home to museums, concert venues, and an outdoor cinema in summer.

SEE

Parc des Buttes-Chaumont

19th

Buttes-Chaumont is one the city's best-kept secrets. And there's little wonder Parisians want to keep this sprawling park to themselves. It's not only one of the largest green spaces but also one of the city's wildest spots, encompassing shady pathways, woody glens, and a spectacular rocky outcrop beneath which waterfalls tumble into an artificial lake. Crowning the park's peak is a delightful Roman-inspired folly, a popular spot for wedding photos, known as the Temple de la Sybille. It's from here that the real highlight unfolds: magnificent views all the way across to the Sacré-Cœur. There are also plenty of gently sloping lawns to picnic on. Also here is the summer-only guinguette, Rosa Bonheur, sister venue to the floating bar beneath the Musée d'Orsay.

Cimetière du Père Lachaise

16 rue du Repos, 20th
Open daily until 6 p.m.

Whether you want to pay your respects to luminaries long departed or simply want to wander its wide and shady avenues, allow at least a few hours to explore Père Lachaise. It's a beautiful cemetery, the largest in Paris, where winding cobbled pathways are lined by plane and maple trees. The myriad tombs and graves here span more than 200 years. Opened in 1804, Père Lachaise has since been expanded several times and is now thought to hold nearly 100,000 graves. Perhaps the most famous are the respective resting places of singers Jim Morrison and Édith Piaf, which have shrine-like status despite efforts of the authori-

PARC DES BUTTES-CHAUMONT

ties to remove votives and graffiti. You can also go in search of literary greats: Oscar Wilde is buried here, as are Gertrude Stein, Richard Wright, and Honoré de Balzac. Pick up a map on your way in to help you find your way around.

Bassin de la Villette
19th

If you walk northeast along the Canal Saint-Martin, you're forced up to street level as you pass Jaurès métro. Navigate the six-road junction and continue in the same direction, and you'll find that what was a narrow waterway suddenly expands into the enormous Bassin de la Villette, the city's largest man-made lake, created in 1808. At first glance it's not particularly beautiful, oblong in shape and lined by wide concrete pathways, but there are plenty of reasons to come. Permanently moored barboats tempt you to stay awhile by the water, while in summer Paris Plages transforms the Bassin with beaches, swimming sections, and perhaps even tea dances along the banks.

Parc de la Villette
19th

There's plenty of green space at the Parc de la Villette. Located at the city's outer reaches, it's only really worth exploring if you're coming for a show, music festival, or exhibition, particularly with kids. This 55-hectare park is a cultural hub, home to the Cité des Sciences et de l'Industrie (Europe's largest science museum) and the Philharmonie de Paris, among other event spaces. Its gardens are beautifully landscaped, a far cry from the abattoirs that once stood here, with 12 thematic areas and play parks for kids. Perhaps the best reason to make a trip is for the summer film festival, when free movies are screened in the open air. The lineup includes plenty of version originale American blockbusters as well as French cinema.

CLOCKWISE FROM TOP LEFT: AUX FOLIES; BASSIN DE LA VILLETTE; RUE SAINTE-MARTHE

Le 50

50 rue de Belleville, 20th
cafesbelleville.com

Coffee roasters Belleville Brûlerie are slowly conquering not just Belleville but all of Paris. Their latest outpost is a drop-in coffee bar in the heart of the 20th arrondissement's Chinatown. Marking the midpoint of rue de Belleville's steep incline, its teal-blue tables and dark wood benches are the perfect spot to pause to sip a coffee and nibble on a madeleine. Or just pick up a café crème to go on your way up the hill to explore Buttes-Chaumont.

La Fontaine de Belleville

31–33 rue Juliette Dodu, 10th
Open daily
cafesbelleville.com

Don't be fooled. La Fontaine might look like any old bistro, but there's more to this sweet little spot than meets the eye. Yes, it has a sidewalk lined with traditional wicker chairs, a classic blue awning, tiled floor, and a mirror-backed bar, but this bar-restaurant has been reinvented by Belleville Brûlerie for a new generation. First and foremost, serious thought has gone into the food and drink. Coffees aren't bitter espressos but lovingly crafted brews made with beans from their own roastery. Ham for their famous jambon-beurre is some of the best in the city. And as well as a no-reservations Sunday brunch, featuring the likes of a dreamy brioche *pain perdu* (French toast), there's live jazz every Saturday afternoon.

PÂTISSERIE

Le Petit Grain

7 rue Denoyez, 20th

Closed Tuesday and Wednesday

lepetitgrainparis.com

Few bakeries see their opening announced in *Vogue*. But this Belleville newcomer has seriously stepped up the area's baking game with inventive breads, cakes, and bakes. The shop's exterior on graffiti-scrawled rue Denoyez is simple and contemporary, and even if you don't stop to buy, you can peek in the floor-to-ceiling windows to watch the bakers at work. But if you go inside, you could find yourself leaving with stacks of sourdough loaves and croissants under your arm or getting sticky fingers while eating miso caramel doughnuts and cinnamon buns straight from the paper bag. It was founded by Brit Edward Delling-Williams, chef of the restaurant Le Grand Bain across the road.

RESTAURANTS

Le Baratin

3 rue Jouye-Rouve, 20th

Closed Sunday and Monday

When the late and great Anthony Bourdain endorsed a no-frills bistro, you know it's going to be good. Le Baratin's chalkboard menu changes daily and the wine list is all natural. You won't find any pretentious plating here, but you will get comforting slow-cooked beef dishes, crispy-skinned roast chicken, and classic entrées like tuna carpaccio. The more adventurous might be tempted to try the calf brain or plump and sweet veal sweetbreads when available. This is still a local spot that is not entirely comfortable with welcoming an international fan club, so book ahead to make sure you get a table. Expect to spend around €40 a head for dinner, and around half that at lunch.

Dilia

1 rue d'Eupatoria, 20th
Closed Tuesday and Wednesday
dilia.fr

Well worth the hike up the hill from Ménilmontant, this inventive Italian restaurant is one of the best in the east of Paris. Exposed brick walls and wildflowers on the tables set the scene for some clever cooking, served as part of two-course formules from €20 at lunch and a range of multicourse tasting menus starting at around €50 for four courses in the evening. Banish any preconceptions about hearty Italian cooking; the dishes are light, delicate, and original. They could include a goat's cheese risotto with capers, bergamot, and mackerel; linguine with anchovies and almonds; or lamb tortellini in a camomile broth. Thanks to a nod in the Michelin Guide, reservations are recommended.

Le Food Market

Boulevard de Belleville, 20th
One Thursday a month, dates vary
lefoodmarket.fr

Street food and food trucks have never really been part of French culture. France is the home of long lunches and gourmet fine dining, and the organizers of Le Food Market were the first to bring this style of eating to the city—albeit with a French twist or two—at their once-a-month event on boulevard de Belleville. Covered stalls are set up down the middle of the road from Ménilmontant to Couronnes from 6 p.m., interspersed with bench seating and perhaps a live band or two. Traders vary each time, so you could find yourself eating boeuf bourguignon in a brioche roll or enjoying a Franco-Canadian take on poutine.

Le Galopin

34 rue Sainte-Marthe, 10th
Closed Saturday and Sunday
le-galopin.com

Set on the little square at the top of rue Sainte-Marthe, Le Galopin is the crowning glory of the neighboring pastel-colored shop fronts. The bare brick walls and typewriter font used on its signage make it look like a relaxed neighborhood bistro, but the food is extraordinary. In the evening go for the tasting menu (around €60), seven artistically plated courses making the most of seasonal produce, perhaps langoustine with avocado, or wagyu beef with asparagus and wild garlic. The brothers behind the restaurant, Romain and Maxime Tischenko, also run La Cave à Michel just down the road, so the natural and biodynamic wine list is superb.

Le Grand Bain

14 rue Denoyez, 20th
Open daily
legrandbainparis.com

With Brit Edward Delling-Williams at the helm, Le Grand Bain has added some much needed upscale dining to an alley better known for spray paint and street art than subtle, scene-defining cooking. The tables are tightly packed and the plates come sharing style, in various sizes from around €15. Perhaps you might get an opportunity to try scallops with dashi and shizo, a magnificently airy chicken liver parfait, or chorizo ravioli. On any given night there'll be at least 10 options to choose from, and staff go out of their way to explain minimal menu descriptions. The bread, of course, is excellent: Its popularity and the opening of boulangerie-pâtisserie Le Petit Grain across the road is no coincidence.

Le Jourdain

101 rue des Couronnes, 20th
Closed Sunday and Monday
lejourdain.fr

If you want to get a feel for a more laid-back side to Belleville, head up the hill above Parc de Belleville to neighborhood bistro Le Jourdain. Lunch menus change daily depending on what's available at the market; dinner is primarily fish dishes served tapas-style from €7, perhaps prawn ravioli with zucchini and ricotta, mackerel with eggplant caviar, or salmon tataki. Wines are affordable and natural, with plenty of bottles below the €30 mark, from zippy Touraine Sauvignons to glugable *vins de soif* (easy-drinking wines) such as Marcel Lapierre's Gamay, Raisins Gaulois.

Palissade

36 rue de Sambre-et-Meuse, 10th
Closed Monday
palissade.biz

Whether you want to sink into a Chesterfield sofa for lunch or perch at the bar for a nightcap well after midnight, this classy but casual all-day neighborhood bar-restaurant is a bit of a Belleville secret. It's slightly off the well-stomped route uphill from the Canal Saint-Martin, and its simple wood cladding certainly doesn't attract attention from the street. This lack of instant curb appeal means you're much more likely to get a table so that you can sample their surprisingly successful Japanese-meets-Breton menu, although book ahead for their wildly popular Sunday brunch.

BARS

Aux Folies

8 rue de Belleville, 20th
Open daily

Nowhere gets as crowded as Aux Folies come apéro hour, when simply every inch of space on the rough-and-ready bar's terrasse is taken up. The appeal? Cheap beers, good vibes, and the chance to stake a claim on one of the prime people-watching spots beneath its iconic neon sign. In the day you'll still see older locals sitting with an espresso and a newspaper; at night a younger crowd takes over, sometimes spilling into rue Denoyez. Its other claim to fame is that Édith Piaf first sang here back in the 1920s, although little of its cabaret past remains today.

La Bellevilloise

19–21 rue Boyer, 20th
Opening times vary
labellevilloise.com

Part bar, part club, part restaurant, part event space, this sprawling hilltop venue has something going on every day of the week. It has a long history as a center of the arts and political thought, founded as a workers' cooperative in 1877. On Friday or Saturday nights, things run late and lines run long for musical lineups ranging from cumbia and Latin to salsa and reggae, perhaps with some live tattooing in a quiet corner for good measure. On Sundays, book ahead for their wildly popular jazz brunch, where you can enjoy an all-you-can-eat buffet in the Halle aux Oliviers accompanied by a live trio or quartet.

At the end of the day, usually from around 6 p.m., café terrasses fill up as everyone gathers to *boire un verre* (have a drink). In summer it's a moment to pause and soak up the sun before thinking about dinner; in winter it's a chance to cozy up under a blanket or heater and reflect on the day. This great tradition takes place all around Paris, everywhere from Saint-Germain's swanky bars to crowded Montmartre cafés, but in Belleville you might feel like a bit more of a local, whether you people watch on boulevard Belleville itself, head to quiet side streets like rue Saint-Marthe, or stop for a glass at a smart wine bar like La Cave de Belleville.

Truth be told, apéro hour is less about where you're drinking but what you're drinking. No matter whether you stay for thirty minutes or three hours, apéro tends to follow the same pattern. This isn't the time for strong cocktails but something light and refreshing. Olives or nuts might turn up unprompted to accompany your drink, or you could order something *à grignoter* (to snack on) like rillettes or saucisson. Sometimes you'll be offered a drink menu, there could be a menu of happy hour offers, or you'll simply be asked what you'd like. Whatever you encounter, you can't go wrong with these five apéritifs in Belleville and beyond.

Rosé: A glass of wine is the simplest apéritif, but let's get one thing straight: in France it's sacrilege to add ice to your wine, except on one very specific occasion. On hot days, if you order a glass of rosé you may request it to be served with a miniature bucket of *glaçons* (ice cubes), which you carefully plop into your glass one at a time with a set of oversized tweezers to keep your drink cool.

Pastis: Anise-flavored pastis is an acquired taste, but once converted you might just find yourself ordering it again and again. The spirit itself is clear, but turns cloudy once water is added. Usually the water is served separately in a carafe, and you mix the two at your table, adding ice cubes if you wish.

Kir: So old-fashioned it's almost cool again, kir is seeing a tentative renaissance. The simplest of cocktails, it's traditionally a splash of *crème de cassis* (blackcurrant liqueur) in a glass of Aligoté, a Burgundian white wine. In practice you'll see various liqueurs on offer, from peach to strawberry, and less-salubrious joints will use up whatever white wine is hanging around. If the white wine is swapped for champagne, it becomes a kir royal.

Craft beer: Paris was slow to join the craft beer bandwagon, but the city is now making up for lost time. In addition to popular beers on tap served as both *demi-pressions* (or *un demi;* half pints) and *pintes* (pints), more and more bars are serving French-brewed craft beers. Just don't expect them to sip them from the bottle; in Paris you'll almost always be given a glass.

A spritz: This Italian favorite is now a firm fixture on the apéro scene. Generally, a spritz is taken to mean one part Aperol, one part prosecco, and one part soda water served with lots of ice—although you might also be offered Aperol's bitter, ruby-red cousin, Campari.

Café Chéri(e)

44 boulevard de la Villette, 19th

Open daily

This scruffy dive bar is a Belleville institution. Its scuffed walls are painted fire-alarm red, with fairy lights snaking around exposed pipes and mosaic mirrors. Outside you sit at repurposed wooden school desks on wobbly plastic chairs. It's the kind of no-fuss spot you can come early for a two-sugars coffee in the sun to shake off last night's hangover, or dance until the early hours with DJs, shots, and super-strong mojitos. Things get busy from around 11 p.m.; come earlier if you're looking for a quiet beer.

La Cave de Belleville

51 rue de Belleville, 19th
Open daily

Standing in contrast to the surrounding shops, La Cave de Belleville is a large modern space, seamlessly combining a shop, deli, and restaurant. You come in off the street to floor-to-ceiling shelves stacked with unusual and exciting bottles; behind are bar seats and tables atmospherically lit with dangling filament light bulbs. Their wine selection is predominantly French and anything but conventional. This is a great place to try a grower champagne or unusual red like Ploussard, grown only in the Jura. Unusually, beer lovers aren't forgotten either, with craft bottles from Paris, Belgium, and beyond. They don't serve full meals, but their planches of cheese and charcuterie are the ideal accompaniment to a tasting session.

Chez Bouboule

26 avenue Jean Aicard, 11th
Closed Sunday and Monday
chezbouboule.fr

Been watching the locals playing pétanque by the canal and ready to give it a whirl? Don't buy your own set of boules, just stop by Chez Bouboule. This dive bar blends beers and bar food with the greatest of all French games. Embrace tradition and sip a Lillet and tonic as you get to grips with the rules on their indoor terrains: two teams compete to throw their boules closest to the *cochonnet* (the jack). You can refuel on Franco-American "tapas" after the match: fries, onion rings, sardine rillettes, and Basque-style pâté. Just don't forget to chalk your name on the board when you arrive to secure your slot on the court.

CLOCKWISE FROM THE TOP: LE PETIT GRAIN; LE PERCHOIR; RUE SAINTE-MARTHE

Combat

63 rue de Belleville, 19th
Open daily

Cool without being pretentious and welcoming without being over-the-top, Combat is one of the best spots in the city for cocktails. It's run by three women—Margot Lecarpentier, Elena Schmitt, and Elise Drouet—who've turned the bar's improbable location into a destination for inventive mixology. Their creations change regularly, including ideas like the Mauzac Glacé (featuring brandy, Pimm's, amontillado sherry, fresh mint, and orange bitters) and the lighter Nardine (a Calvados, egg white, and lime combination scattered with dried rose petals).

Paname Brewing Company

41bis quai de la Loire, 19th
Daily until 2 a.m.
panamebrewingcompany.com

A microbrewery with a mega view, Paname Brewing Company occupies a huge refurbished warehouse at the top of the Bassin de la Villette, with glorious views over the water from its floating terrace. This bar, restaurant, and brewery is only a few years old, but they mean business. They brew five signature beers on-site—including an IPA, saison, and lager—plus some punchy specials such as 9% ABV coffee ale. The menu is mostly American bar food, so expect burgers, pizza, and quesadillas mixed in with a few nonnegotiable French essentials: charcuterie platters and steak-frites. For non-beer drinkers, there are wines by the glass and cocktails.

Le Perchoir

14 rue Crespin du Gast, 11th
Open daily

Le Perchoir offers everything you could possibly want from a slightly pretentious rooftop bar: an unmarked entrance with an unnecessary red rope to keep the line in check, strong cocktails, and stupendous views. That said, the staff are generally lovely and the drinks reasonably priced at €12 to €15 a pop. Get there early to stake out one of the outdoor sofas and sip on Moscow Mules and negronis as you watch the sun go down over the city's rooftops. You can even see across to the Sacré-Cœur. There's a restaurant downstairs if you find a couple of hours of posing really works up an appetite.

Point Éphémère

200 quai de Valmy, 10th
Daily from noon
pointephemere.org

This grungy canal-side warehouse venue has been a much-loved part of the Paris nightlife scene for years. There's a club (buy tickets in advance for gigs and DJs), bar, exhibition space, and summertime rooftop terrace—but you could quite happily just come to drink beers in plastic cups by the water's edge. It's just north of the heart of the action on the Canal Saint-Martin, on a graffiti-lined stretch just before it turns into the Bassin de la Villette. It's open from lunchtime, and if you turn up early you'll find that the vibe is surprisingly chilled out.

Le Renard Bar

38 rue de Sambre-et-Meuse, 10th
Closed Sunday
animaux.bar

Signature drinks for less than €10 and happy hour until 9 p.m. are the big appeals at this small but cool cocktail bar. Take inspiration from the bar's name (*renard* means fox), and try a What the Fox with tequila, grapefruit, lime, and cranberry; or go for something punchier like a rum-based Point Vert with peach liqueur. If you'd rather stay in familiar territory, there are plenty of classics, too: pisco sours, negronis, daiquiris, and virgin mojitos. The same team also runs the excellent L'Ours Bar near Gare de l'Est.

CHAPTER 8

Saint-Germain and the Latin Quarter

When Parisians refer to the Left Bank, they mean Saint-Germain and the Latin Quarter, renowned as the city's literary heart and home to some of its most elegant neighborhoods. Today, these are among the most expensive parts of the city to live, shop, and eat; but little vestiges of their countercultural history remain. Jean-Paul Sartre and Simone de Beauvoir wrote here, as did Camus, while Picasso and Renoir both lived and painted on the Left Bank. Many Americans also contributed to the notoriety of these neighborhoods: Gertrude Stein held her literary salons in her home on rue de Fleurus, Hemingway wrote and drank in many of Saint-Germain's cafés and bistros, and Julia Child mastered the art of French cooking on rue de l'Universite (or Roo de Loo as she called it).

There's no better place to get a feel for Saint-Germain than the genteel Jardin du Luxembourg where you can join locals for a stroll by the miniature lake. The streets to the north are shopping and dining heaven. Buzzy rue de Seine has some of the most laid-back bars, restaurants, and galleries, while boulevard Saint-Germain is lined with one-time literary haunts including Café de Flore and Les Deux Magots. Le Bon Marché, off boulevard Raspail, is the city's top department store, while the street itself hosts an organic market on Sundays.

To the west is foreign embassy territory, which would feel a little soulless were it not for a few superb museums. The Musée Rodin displays some of the artist's greatest works in an 18th-century mansion surrounded by a statue-filled garden; it's among the city's best small museums. On a much grander scale is the simply enormous Musée de l'Armée, an imposing museum dedicated to military history. It also houses Napoleon's tomb.

To the east, Saint-Germain seamlessly merges into the Latin Quarter. Its spiritual center is the Sorbonne University, a hub of student life, especially along rue Mouffetard. There are more tombs of note in the magnificent Panthéon, whose crypt holds the remains of France's most revered figures including Victor Hugo and Marie Curie. You can take a step much further back in time at the Musée de Cluny, dedicated to the Middle Ages,

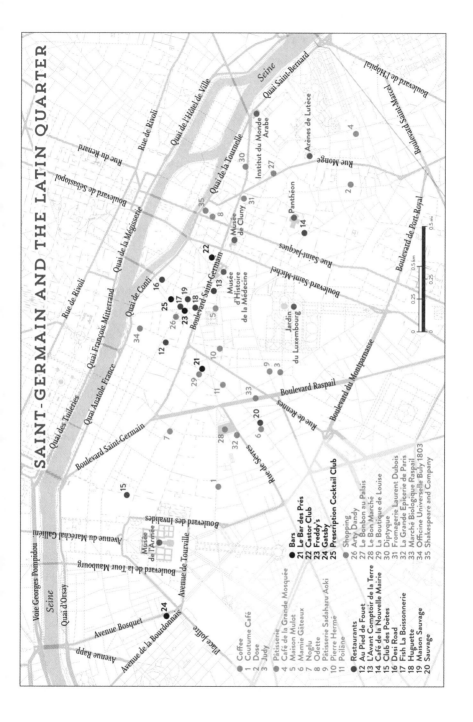

SAINT-GERMAIN AND THE LATIN QUARTER

Coffee
1 Coutume Café
2 Dose
3 Judy

Pâtisserie
4 Café de la Grande Mosquée
5 Maison Mulot
6 Mamie Gâteaux
7 Noglu
8 Odette
9 Pâtisserie Sadaharu Aoki
10 Pierre Hermé
11 Poilâne

Restaurants
12 Au Pied de Fouet
13 L'Avant Comptoir de la Terre
14 Café de la Nouvelle Mairie
15 Club des Poètes
16 Desi Road
17 Fish La Boissonnerie
18 Huguette
19 Maison Sauvage
20 Sauvage

Bars
21 Le Bar des Prés
22 Castor Club
23 Freddy's
24 Gatsby
25 Prescription Cocktail Club

Shopping
26 Arty Dandy
27 Le Bonbon au Palais
28 Le Bon Marché
29 La Boutique de Louise
30 Diptyque
31 Fromagerie Laurent Dubois
32 La Grande Épicerie de Paris
33 Marché Biologique Raspail
34 Officine Universelle Buly 1803
35 Shakespeare and Company

or go even further back at the Arènes de Lutèce, the remains of a Roman amphitheater rediscovered in the late 1800s.

Whatever season it happens to be, don't miss a stroll in the beautiful Jardin des Plantes by the river. It's abutted by two fascinating sights quite different to those in the rest of the quartier: the Grande Mosquée de Paris, which has a lovely courtyard café, and the superb Institut du Monde Arabe, which shines light on the history and culture of the Arab world.

SEE

Jardin du Luxembourg

6th

Just like the Jardin des Tuileries, the Jardin du Luxembourg has a long and fascinating history—but unlike the Tuileries, it's still very much a community space today. Tai chi is practiced in the shadier groves, its tennis courts are packed in the summer, and toy sailboats are raced by kids on the garden's famous lake at the weekend. The garden was first laid out in 1612 by Queen Marie de' Medici, and her Florentine-inspired mix of formal avenues, rose gardens, hidden ponds, and orchards is just as delightful today. There's little in the way of grass to sprawl out on, but lots of gravel paths to wander—and you can pull up one of the garden's distinctive green chairs in your favorite spot.

Musée de l'Armée

129 rue de Grenelle, 7th
Open daily
musee-armee.fr

Occupying the Hôtel des Invalides, built as a hospital for wounded soldiers, the Musée de l'Armée commemorates France's military history. It's simply enormous, so don't just drop in expecting to see the highlights. In all there are seven collections here, including artillery, mostly displayed outdoors in the courtyard, and armor and weaponry dating back

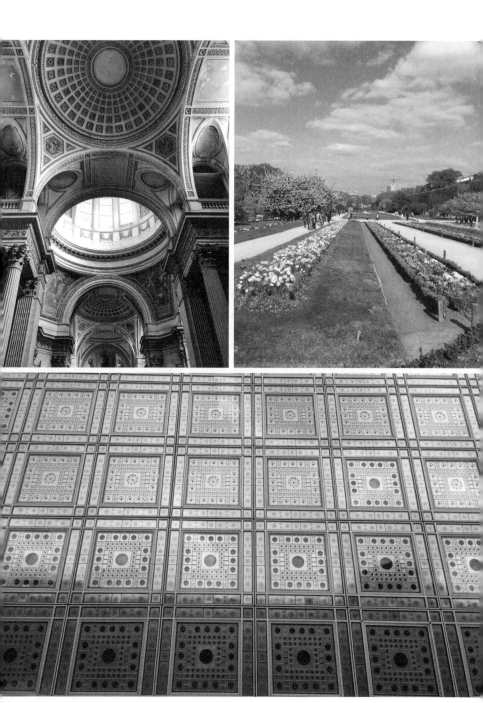

CLOCKWISE FROM TOP LEFT: INSIDE THE PANTHEON; JARDIN DES PLANTES; INSTITUT DU MONDE ARABE

to the 13th century. For many, Napoleon I's tomb in the golden Dôme des Invalides is reason enough to come. As Les Invalides' defining feature, it was built in the late 1600s as a royal chapel by Louis XIV, with Napoleon's ashes interred here following his state funeral in 1861. The Dôme is intentionally separated from the Cathedral of Saint-Louis des Invalides, the veteran's chapel, which is still the official cathedral of the French army.

Musée de Cluny

28 rue Du Sommerard, 5th
Closed Tuesday
musee-moyenage.fr

It might be oh so tempting to pass up a museum of medieval history for better-known collections, but miss this paean to the Moyen Âge (previously known as the Musée National du Moyen Âge) and you're seriously missing out. Not only is it improbably sited on a Roman frigidarium (once part of a larger bath house), which you can explore as part of your visit, it's also home to the simply magnificent *La Dame à la Licorne (The Lady with the Unicorn)*. This set of six tapestries depicts the five senses, plus a sixth one mysteriously named *À Mon Seul Désir (My Sole Desire)*. Dating from the 15th century, it's often referred to as the *Mona Lisa* of the Middle Ages. Extensive renovations are set to transform the museum by the end of 2020, so just bear in mind that there may be some disruption to opening hours and limited access at times until the work is complete.

Panthéon

Place du Panthéon, 5th
Open daily
paris-pantheon.fr

It's hard to comprehend that this magnificent mausoleum was first built as a church, admittedly one that its architect, Jacques-Germain Soufflot, envisaged as dwarfing St. Peter's in Rome and St. Paul's in London. He certainly succeeded in these lofty ambitions, but in the end its use

INSIDE THE PANTHEON

for religious services was short lived. After the Revolution it was transformed into a panthéon, a place to commemorate and honor the nation's heroes, a purpose it still fulfills today. Above ground you can wander beneath its astonishing domes and frescoes, and admire Foucault's Pendulum, a re-creation of the device the physicist used to prove the Earth's constant rotation in 1851. In the crypt lie the remains of French heroes ranging from Voltaire and Victor Hugo to Marie Curie and Simone Veil, their work brought to life by interactive displays.

Arènes de Lutèce
rue Monge, 5th
Open daily

Paris is full of surprises, although it's hard to imagine just how much of a shock the discovery of this partially preserved Roman arena must have been in 1896, when it was dug up during works to make way for the construction of rue Monge. It was later restored in 1917 (thanks to the efforts of Victor Hugo, among others) and today offers a little glimpse into a very different era of Parisian history—one that you little come across in the city's great museums and galleries. The amphitheater is thought to have been constructed in the first century AD and may have seated up to 15,000 spectators, although you can only imagine that gladiators once fought here.

Institut du Monde Arabe
1 rue des Fossés Saint-Bernard, 5th
Closed Monday
imarabe.org

Part library, part exhibition space, part gallery, the Institut du Monde Arabe offers an unrivaled insight into the history of the Arab world. The permanent collection isn't the most logical to explore for non-French speakers, but its blend of artifacts, calligraphy, ceramics, and multimedia—examining Islam, Christianity, and Judaism in turn—is well worth a visit. Superb temporary exhibitions cover subjects as diverse as photography and hip hop to the history of Palestine and Islam in Africa. There's nowhere else like it in Europe. The building is just as memorable: Its southern facade is covered in 240 intricate metal mashrabiyas. Architect Jean Nouvel reinvented this traditional latticework feature with a modern twist: Each one is controlled by photoelectric cells that adjust the light let inside. Stop for a mint tea in the courtyard to admire his mastery.

Musée d'Histoire de la Médecine

12 rue de l'École de Médecine, 6th
Afternoons only, closed Thursday and Sunday

Part of the Université Paris Descartes, the Museum of the History of Medicine preserves some of the oldest medical instruments in Europe—including some dating back to the 16th century. It's a slightly macabre collection without much in the way of explanation, so your imagination is left to run wild as you examine somewhat unsettling kits of surgical tools and primitive metal prosthetics. If you speak a little French, or have a passing knowledge of basic medical practice, you're likely to get more from your visit. Regardless, at less than €5 to enter it's still worth popping in.

COFFEE

Coutume Café

47 rue de Babylone, 7th
Open daily
coutumecafe.com

Specialty coffee shops are thin on the ground in the 6th and 7th, so this spacious café is wildly popular. Upon seeing its filament light bulbs and Pyrex lab beakers, you could be forgiven for expecting style over substance, but Coutume is warm and friendly. Cakes, cookies, and raspberry-studded financiers complement the coffees, plus there's a small choice of organic wines and craft beer. Helpfully, they also offer coffees to take away—a rarity, as staying caffeinated on the go is still a little-adopted habit on the Left Bank.

Dose

73 rue Mouffetard, 5th
Closed Monday
dosedealerdecafe.fr

Tucked in the entrance to a passageway off rue Mouffetard, amid countless hole-in-the-wall crêperies, this specialty coffee spot counters jambon-fromage overload with matcha lattes, made-to-order juices, and plenty of cookies, muffins, and brownies. It was started by two cousins who were inspired by time spent in London's barista-led coffee shops and decided to re-create the atmosphere back home—with an emphasis on French products. In need of a serious pick-me-up? Try their Valrhona hot chocolate topped with whipped cream. They also have a second address in the 17th.

Judy

18 rue de Fleurus, 6th
Open daily
judy-paris.com

Let's get one thing straight: Judy might look like a pretty Saint-Germain corner café with its candy-striped awnings, but it's not really a local spot. Yet what it lacks in newspaper-reading Parisians and flaky croissants it makes up for in a menu of cold-pressed juices, almond-milk coffees, avocado on toast, and Buddha bowls designed by an Australian naturopath. All the ingredients are organic, and unlike in many of the city's restaurants, vegans and those following a gluten- or lactose-free diet will find plenty of options. The only downside is the price: You can easily spend €25 on a light breakfast.

PÂTISSERIE

Café de la Grande Mosquée

47 rue Geoffroy-Saint-Hilaire, 5th

Open daily

The beautiful Hispano-Moresque arches of the Grande Mosquée de Paris, built in the 1920s and inspired in part by the Alhambra in Granada, Spain, are among the architectural highlights of the Latin Quarter. You can visit the mosque itself, but most people round the corner from the main entrance and head to the courtyard café, where mosaic tables are set beneath canopies and lanterns, sometimes in a cloud of shisha smoke. Waiters bring around trays laden with glasses of hot and sugary *thé à la menthe* (mint tea), which you don't order but simply request from afar with a nod, handing over €2 each time. On the way in, stop at the counter for sticky North African pâtisseries, eaten on paper plates.

Maison Mulot

76 rue de Seine, 6th

Open daily

maison-mulot.com

This Left Bank pâtisserie *par excellence* was once the empire of legend Gérard Mulot, who passed the reins over to Fabien Rouillard a few years ago. He's proved a worthy successor. Their macarons are one of the big attractions, ranging in flavors from coffee to strawberry and champagne, and they're sold in full and miniature sizes: handy when you just can't choose. Then there are the chocolates, airy fraisiers, nougat-laden mille-feuilles, and vanilla éclairs. You name it, they make it to perfection. They also sell baguettes, croissants, and sandwiches, but don't make them the main event.

Mamie Gâteaux

66 rue du Cherche-Midi, 6th
Closed Sunday and Monday

For afternoon tea in Saint-Germain, it's all about Mamie Gâteaux. Their wide selection of sweet treats is suitably eclectic, spanning English-style scones to slices of fluffy American-style lemon meringue pie. They could have gone overboard on the cutesy décor. Instead it's more country kitchen than chintzy tearoom, a welcome contrast to the formality of hotel tearooms that dominate this scene. There are plenty of teas to choose from, of course, but the hot chocolate is really special.

Noglu

69 rue de Grenelle, 7th
Open daily
noglu.fr

In a city not renowned for its approach to catering for food allergies, Noglu is somewhat of a savior for celiacs and anyone on a restricted diet. You can still tuck into delicious brioches, madeleines, matcha cakes, and brownies at this daytime eat-in or take-out café, but all ingredients are organic and gluten-free. More filling savory options include grilled cheese sandwiches and quiches, plus there are coffees and hot chocolates made with almond, coconut, or soy milk. Their other branch, in the Passage des Panoramas in the 2nd arrondissement, has more of a restaurant vibe and is open into the evenings.

Odette

77 rue Galande, 5th
Open daily
odette-paris.com

Odette might be on the Left Bank, but one of the biggest attractions of stopping here to pick up a boîte de choux is the views north across the river to Île de la Cité. This tiny pâtisserie makes some of the best cream puffs in the city, which you can eat at their outdoor tables in summer, have inside in their in tiny salon de thé, or take away in a picnic-ready box. Flavors range from fruity options like lemon and passion fruit to rich praline and coffee options. A box of nine costs around €16.

Pâtisserie Sadaharu Aoki

35 rue de Vaugirard, 6th
Closed Monday
sadaharuaoki.com

Superstar Japanese pâtissier Sadaharu Aoki might have more bakeries in Tokyo than Paris these days, but he's been working in France since the 1990s and his fusion pâtisserie creations are renowned. Classics like vanilla millefeuilles get a sprinkling of matcha powder, choux puffs are filled with green tea crème mousseline, and macarons come flavored with yuzu and black sesame. His rue de Vaugirard shop is tiny, but it's just around the corner from the Jardin du Luxembourg, so you won't have to carry your boxes of delicate treats too far before you tuck in.

Pierre Hermé

72 rue Bonaparte, 6th
Open daily
pierreherme.com

One name is synonymous with macarons in Paris: Pierre Hermé. These days you'll see his creations everywhere from the UAE to Disneyland (he created Mickey Mouse's 90th birthday cake), but they're best sampled in his home city. Forget about the classics and go for seasonal specials: the Ispahan (rose, lychee, and raspberry); the Enchanted Garden (lime, raspberry, and pepper); or the Satine (cream cheese with orange and passion fruit compote). Expect a box of seven macarons to set you back around €20. You can also sample his signature chocolates and delicate pâtisserie creations—his puff pastry (perhaps a praline and hazelnut 2000 Feuilles) is always a good choice.

Poilâne

8 rue du Cherche-Midi, 6th
Closed Sunday
poilane.com

For many years Poilâne breads were the standard by which all others in the city were measured. Pierre Poilâne founded the now world-famous bakery on this spot in 1932. Three generations later it's run by New York–born Apollonia Poilâne, who took the helm when she was just a teenager. She upholds the same principals of their sourdough bread-making traditions: loaves made from stone-milled flours, without additives, baked on-site in a wood-fired oven. The round, thick-crusted miche Poilâne is the classic, but once you've tried the original you could move onto their soft and airy pain de mie, signature punition butter cookies, deep-golden croissants, and *chaussons aux pommes* (apple turnovers).

A BEGINNER'S GUIDE TO PÂTISSERIE

You could spend months in Paris and still find new cakes and pastries to discover. Every bakery has their specialty, but there are a few must-try options. You'll spot them in almost every bakery and chichi tea-room, and on many dessert menus.

Chausson aux pommes: The French version of an apple turnover, made with *pâte feuilletée* (puff pastry) and generously filled with apple compote.

Opera: The pick of the bunch for lovers of dark and intense desserts, these individual rectangular cakes are formed from multiple thin layers of coffee-infused joconde sponge, coffee cream, and rich chocolate ganache.

Saint-Honoré: Few agree exactly where in Paris the Saint-Honoré was invented, but this cake is a Parisian classic, a puff pastry base topped with vanilla cream and miniature choux buns.

Baba au rhum: Somewhere between a brioche bun and a doughnut, the baba is a delicate yet doughy delight—even more so when drenched in rum and topped with Chantilly cream.

Millefeuille: At its most basic a millefeuille, sometimes known as a Napoleon, is made from layers of compacted puff pastry and flour-thickened crème pâtissière. You'll also see versions pimped with caramel, fresh fruit, or chocolate.

Fraisier: If you're visiting Paris when strawberry season is in full swing, you have to try one of these strawberry cakes. Either square or round, the layers of fruit liquor–soaked génoise sponge, thick and rich crème mousseline, and fresh strawberries are irresistible.

Madeleines: Light and fluffy madeleines—always baked in distinctive shell-shaped molds—are synonymous with Paris. Made with just butter, sugar, flour, and eggs, although sometimes flavored with lemon zest, they're proof that the simplest recipes can be the most delicious.

Kouign-amann: Hailing from Brittany, this sweet, buttery, and flaky pastry cake has something of a cult following. It has a texture all its own: softer than puff pastry and more sugary and dense than a croissant.

Religieuse: A religieuse is simply one small profiterole perched atop a larger one. They're usually filled with cream and often topped with chocolate sauce or salted caramel.

Mont Blanc: Named after France's tallest mountain, this bubble-shaped cake comprises a meringue topped with chestnut purée and whipped cream. Many bakeries alter the recipe to create their own unique take each fall.

Paris-Brest: This wheel-shaped choux pastry, filled with praline cream and topped with almonds, was created to celebrate the Paris–Brest cycle race. Eat with care to avoid getting covered in cream.

Chouquettes: On a budget? Pick up a bag of chouquettes, airy choux puffs studded with pearl sugar, sold in almost every boulangerie across Paris.

RESTAURANTS

L'Avant Comptoir de la Terre

3 Carrefour de l'Odéon, 6th

Open daily

Part of the mini empire of Yves Camdeborde, considered by many to be one of the founders of bistronomy, this standing-only tapas bar (there's not a single seat) joins his acclaimed restaurant Le Comptoir du Relais and next-door seafood bar L'Avant Comptoir de la Mer on the Carrefour de l'Odéon. The menu dangles from the ceiling in a forest of laminated photo cards depicting the likes of foie gras with figs, ham croquettes, charcuterie, and slow-braised pork belly. You can point and pick the dishes if you wish, but it's better to strike up a conversation with the bar staff, who'll recommend the best choices and the perfect wine pairings. Bread will arrive as soon as you squeeze yourself into a little spot to eat, as well as a soccer ball–sized mound of butter, which guests slowly share and deplete as the evening wears on.

Café de la Nouvelle Mairie

19 rue des Fossés Saint-Jacques, 5th

Closed Saturday and Sunday

Great food in France is often about the art of simplicity. In this whirlwind of a bistro, that's exactly what they specialize in: classic dishes (from €20) that sound uncomplicated but taste superb. Some are hearty (think sausage with lentils or steak topped with caramelized shallots); others are as simple as heirloom tomatoes with olive oil and ricotta di bufala. Tables are tightly squeezed together, both inside and on the sidewalk, and you order from the day's chalkboard menus that are propped up on the nearest bench or windowsill for you to peruse. Wines are natural, beers are craft brews, and coffees are as bitter as they come. In short, it's everything you could want from contemporary and informal bistro dining in Paris—and it's just steps from the Panthéon.

Club des Poètes

30 rue de Bourgogne, 7th
Irregular hours, closed Sunday

What do you get if you cross an alternative poetry club with an old-fashioned restaurant? Club des Poètes defies definition. Low-lit and sleepy at any time of the day, this delightful time capsule transitions from bistro to literary salon with ease. Come at lunch for a plat du jour (there may be only two or three options for around €15, and they're likely to be meaty) or arrive in the evening to hear recitations of everything from Baudelaire to Rimbaud. If the mood takes you, you can even recite your own choice of verse.

Desi Road

14 rue Dauphine, 6th
Open daily
desiroadrestaurant.com

Swap croissants for curries at this bijou restaurant located moments from the river on the Left Bank. It's one of the best spots for authentic Indian cuisine in the city. Their short but sweet menu ranges from tandoori lamb chops to homemade rotis, but the highlights are definitely the thalis—a selection of different curries, including all-vegetarian options, served traditionally in small metal bowls with rice, dal, and dessert on the same tray. With thalis around the €25 mark it's not particularly cheap, but well worth a little splurge.

Fish La Boissonnerie

69 rue de Seine, 6th
Open daily
fishlaboissonnerie.com

Don't be misled by the name. The focus at this laid-back, exposed-walled restaurant isn't fish, but modern French cuisine paired with interesting wines. Their wine list is a thing of beauty—heavy on the Loire, Jura, and

Beaujolais—with plenty below the €40 mark. The association with the sea ends at the mosaic exterior, where orange-tiled fish leap either side of the arched picture window. Instead you could find pork belly with cherries and almonds, delicate slow-cooked beef cheeks, or even interesting pasta dishes. Expect to pay around €25 for two courses at lunch and up to double that at dinner. It might look casual, but the attentive, warm service and top-quality ingredients give away that some serious cooking is going on here. It's run by the same team behind Freddy's bar, on the other side of the street, and their bread is baked daily across the road.

Huguette

81 rue de Seine, 6th
Open daily
huguette-bistro.com

Slurping down a half-dozen huîtres with a glass of Muscadet is a classic French gastronomic experience. And there are few better spots to indulge in a platter of freshly shucked oysters than beneath Huguette's blue-and-white striped awnings on the pretty, café-lined rue de Seine. This bistro has a distinctly Breton theme, and thanks to the heated pavement tables, you might just feel transported to the seaside without leaving central Paris. If you really want to get into a seafood feast, try *crevettes grises* (grey shrimp), *bulots* (whelks), or a whole grilled *homard* (lobster). For the less traditional, there are ceviche, poke bowls, and gyoza. Expect to spend more than €30 a head on food.

Maison Sauvage

5 rue de Buci, 6th
Open daily
maison-sauvage.fr

Rue de Buci is everything you imagine Saint-Germain to be: a quaint, narrow street lined by sidewalk cafés that stay lively from first thing in the morning until well past midnight. Maison Sauvage is the pick of the bunch for atmosphere. They make the most of their prime corner plot by draping their awnings in boughs of flowers, with trailing vines laced around the windows above. Stake out an outdoor table for brunch, lunch, dinner, or drinks to watch the world go by. The menu has a vaguely healthy angle, ranging from ricotta toast and granola in the morning to caesar salads, crispy cauliflower, and salmon-avocado tartare later in the day (mains around €15–20).

Au Pied de Fouet

45 rue de Babylone, 7th
Closed Sunday
aupieddefouet.fr

This bistro is as old-fashioned as they come. Red-check tablecloths and paper place settings set the scene. The walls are hung higgledy-piggledy with photos, prints, and signs. And you sit up close to your neighbors, either on the ground floor or in a little mezzanine barely visible from the street. Dishes are hearty and traditional: start with pâté de campagne or *oeuf dur mayonnaise* (similar to deviled eggs); move on to confit de canard; then finish with a rich, sweet dessert like tarte tatin or a chocolate fondant. The only surprise is the price: You can order three courses for just €20. There's also a sister restaurant nearby in the 6th.

Sauvage

55 rue du Cherche-Midi, 6th
Closed Monday

The food and wines at this stripped back and very un-Saint-Germain spot are superb—whether you drop by the relaxed wine bar or eat in the full restaurant directly opposite across the road. Plats vary in size (up to €30) and are bold in flavor and presentation, perhaps duck hearts with wild garlic, crispy sweetbreads with cabbage, or even tuna with strawberries. Ask for advice on wine pairings: You could find yourself trying a soft and fruity Cabernet Franc, a Grolleau blend from Anjou, or one of Sylvain Bock's unusual whites from the Ardèche. (Note: despite the name, Sauvage has no connection to the nearby Maison Sauvage.)

CLOCKWISE FROM THE TOP: L'AVANT COMPTOIR DE LA TERRE; GATSBY; CAFÉ DE LA NOUVELLE MAIRIE

BARS

Le Bar des Prés

25 rue du Dragon, 6th
Open daily
lebardespres.com

There's a hint of noughties New York about this sleek Saint-Germain bar. Perhaps it's the pricey sushi menu (sashimi, maki, and California rolls served with yuzu-infused soy sauce), the low-lit booths, and the vodka-heavy cocktail list. Yet this spot has some serious French pedigree, as it's part of renowned chef Cyril Lignac's ever-growing empire. If you fancy getting dressed up for an evening sipping sake—or perhaps a couple of glasses of Billecart-Salmon champagne—it's the only place to come.

Castor Club

14 rue Hautefeuille, 6th
Closed Sunday

Peek through the mailbox slit in the door to see if there's space in this tiny cocktail bar, where there's room for just one line of drinkers at the bar and another side-by-side in nooks along the wood-paneled back wall. It feels a little bit like stepping into the hull of a boat, especially if you order an Aye Aye Captain Cap (gin, lime juice, blueberry, and vanilla), although the tequila-based Jalisco Moon (with Chartreuse, rosemary syrup, and apricot) is one of the highlights of the menu. All cocktails are around the €15 mark, and on busy nights you can stay on for dancing in the cellar.

Freddy's

54 rue de Seine, 6th
Open daily

Usually crowded, loud, and welcoming, Freddy's is the kind of wine bar where you feel like a regular the moment you walk in the door. It's decidedly un-snooty and feels slightly out of place in Saint-Germain with its no-reservation policy and natural-wine-heavy drinks list. While at sister restaurant Semilla next door you can easily spend upward of €150 on dinner for two, Freddy's is affordable and laid-back. Stop for a glass of wine (from around €6) or cancel your dinner plans and get carried away ordering plate-upon-plate of tapas until you're ready to pop. Try the zucchini beignets, padrón peppers, and definitely non-tapas-sized plates like onglet with chimichurri.

Gatsby

64 avenue Bosquet, 7th
Open daily
legatsby.fr

Sipping an old fashioned at a just-themed-enough tribute to F. Scott Fitzgerald's greatest novel is about as close to the 1920s as you can get in Paris today. From the heavy-cut crystal glassware to the gramophone displayed behind the cozy leather booths, this speakeasy does golden-age glamour without being pretentious—although bookworms might note that the wallpaper matches the gold-embossed jacket of Penguin's special edition titles. If a classic cocktail doesn't take your fancy, you could try a Daisy (vodka with lime, strawberry purée, pineapple juice, and tonic) or a Myrtle (gin with bitters, passion fruit purée, and apple juice). The unshockable should test their French by reading the reproduction brothel "menu" framed on the wall.

Prescription Cocktail Club

23 rue Mazarine, 6th
Open daily

Another triumph from the Experimental Cocktail Club team, this Saint-Germain cocktail bar has plenty of old-school Left-Bank cool. Its two candlelit floors are open late every night, until 4 a.m. on Friday and Saturday, and it's held a spot on the World's Best Bars list for years. Think of it as the grande dame of the city's speakeasies: easy going and gimmick free.

You won't find any secret doors here, but you will get marvelous cocktails for around €15 a pop; try their very old Cuban (rum, champagne, ginger cordial, bitters, mint, and lime) or get lost in their whisky collection.

SHOPPING

Arty Dandy

1 rue de Furstemberg, 6th
Open daily
artydandy.com

A concept store with a simple motto, to help you live life with style and panache, Arty Dandy will stock your wardrobe with everything you need to become a modern-day dandy, whatever your gender. Start with leather sneakers from Parisian brand Bons Baisers de Paname, emblazoned with words like *bisou* (kiss) or *amour* (love), add an embroidered slogan tee from Maison Labiche, and top off your look with a cross-body bag from Tammy & Benjamin or a Bleu de Chauffe satchel. Expect international appearances from brands like Gentlemen's Hardware, purveyor of handy travel grooming kits, and Marshall radios, a hipster essential that knows no borders.

Le Bonbon au Palais

19 rue Monge, 5th
Closed Sunday and Monday
lebonbonaupalais.com

This busy boulevard might not be where you'd expect to find a delightfully old-fashioned candy shop, less one recommended by the mayor of Paris herself. Every treat in this store is made in France, from the homemade marshmallows—worlds away from the shop-bought variety you squish into a s'more—to Léon Mazet's sophisticated yuzu pralines. Bakers might be tempted by crystalized mint leaves or candied orange, and there are plenty of hard candies to suck as you sightsee. They display their wares in glass bell jars, and your selection will be carefully put together by gloved staff.

Le Bon Marché

24 rue de Sèvres, 7th
Open daily
24sevres.com

Le Bon Marché is to Paris what Bergdorf Goodman is to New York. The city's first department store, opened in 1852, it's long been the chicest spot for luxury shopping. Now owned by LVMH, this temple to style stocks everything from high fashion and elegant homewares to beautifully crafted luggage and stationary. It's a Left Bank landmark, and one that's worth visiting just to admire the window displays and to take a ride on the white-tile escalators designed by Andrée Putman, even if you're not intending to shop. Large-scale art installations have also been a feature ever since the store first opened, with past collaborations featuring work by Chiharu Shiota, Ai Weiwei, Edoardo Tresoldi, and Leandro Erlich.

La Boutique de Louise

32 rue du Dragon, 6th
Closed Sunday
laboutiquedelouise.com

Even cacti get a cutesy twist in this Saint-Germain boutique that's stocked with affordable but unique accessories and decorations from carefully selected brands. Browse through delicate gold bracelets, oh-so-casually layered by Parisians to complete their "I just threw this on" look, or dangly mix-and-match geometric earrings. On the homewares front, expect the likes of *kawaii* (adorable) Sass & Belle mugs, quirky wall stickers, and those cute cacti, packaged in unusual, colorful tins. If you're in the market for gifts, stock up on cards and notepads, and look out for sweet ideas for new parents like star-print muslins.

Diptyque

34 boulevard Saint-Germain, 5th
Closed Sunday
diptyqueparis.com

If there's one French fragrance brand you're likely to have heard of back home, it's perfumer and candle-maker Diptyque, founded in Paris in 1961. This was their first boutique, and its address even now is used as the name for one of their signature lines. Their delicately scented slow-burning candles, all with distinctive yet classy black-and-white type designs, are the most popular products—but there's plenty more besides. These days their collection ranges from miniature fragrance diffusers, shower gels, and body lotions to textiles and stationary.

Fromagerie Laurent Dubois

47 ter boulevard Saint-Germain, 5th
Closed Monday
fromageslaurentdubois.fr

Whether you're in search of a special goat's, cow's or ewe's milk cheese—or simply in pursuit of utter gluttony—don't miss a trip to this fantastic fromagerie. Choosing a cheese here is not as simple as picking it off the shelf: First you discuss your tastes with the staff, then if you're lucky you might even get a sample to try before you buy. It's best not to come with too definite an idea of what you're after. Instead, let yourself be led by their expertise. You might leave with a bleu des causses, similar to Roquefort, a beautifully creamy wedge of brie, or fresh goat's cheese with figs. Whatever you pick, you won't be disappointed. Owner Laurent Dubois is a Meilleur Ouvrier de France, a title awarded only to France's finest culinary craftsmen.

La Grande Epicerie de Paris

38 rue de Sèvres, 7th
Open daily
lagrandeepicerie.com

Food heaven in Paris can take many forms. If you're looking to go home with a suitcase more heavily laden than when you arrived, you might want to consider a trip to the Grande Epicerie. This upscale emporium, part of Le Bon Marché, has whole aisles devoted to French specialties, from chocolates and teas to mustards and jams. Others are stacked with international imports: pomegranate molasses and orange-blossom water from Lebanon, beautifully packed Italian pasta, and somewhat more prosaic staples like baked beans and maple syrup. Then there's the fresh fruit, vegetables, cheese, and meat. Just beware that buying ingredients for dinner here might just empty your bank account, and if you are buying treats to take home, be sure to check border regulations about what's permitted.

Marché Biologique Raspail

Boulevard Raspail, 6th
Sunday 9 a.m. to 3 p.m.

The scent of herbs, soap, and freshly squeezed orange juice fills the air at this fancy organic market, which sets up every Sunday on boulevard Raspail. As you might expect, given the area's wealthy denizens, it's a cut above some of Paris's weekly markets in terms of produce and price. If you're staying in an apartment with a kitchen, this market presents the opportunity to pick up some beautiful cheese and a bottle of wine. If you're just passing through, there are just-baked pains au chocolat to munch as you browse beautiful displays of flowers, vegetables, and Provençal beauty products.

Officine Universelle Buly 1803

6 rue Bonaparte, 6th
Closed Sunday
buly1803.com

Don't be put off by their wordy name; l'Officine Universelle Buly are about one thing only: beauté. This skin care brand might have been founded in 1803, and these days have outlets in Tokyo and Taipei, but a visit to their Parisian boutique is a magical experience. In their old-school perfumery, tradition and ingenuity are beautifully intertwined. Essentials include their Pommade Virginale face cream and damask rose body oil, but even the more modern additions like micellar cleansing water come in gorgeous imitation antique bottles. Looking for something a bit more original? Try coriander-cucumber dental floss or English-honey soap in a customized box.

Shakespeare and Company

37 rue de la Bûcherie, 5th
Open daily
shakespeareandcompany.com

This literary landmark might just be the most famous English-language bookstore in the world. Its first location at 12 rue de l'Odéon, run by Sylvia Beach, was central in the lives of the Lost Generation. It's where Ernest Hemingway, Gertrude Stein, and F. Scott Fitzgerald famously browsed for inspiration. After it was closed during the war, George Whitman opened his own shop in tribute, and Shakespeare and Company's second incarnation was born at 37 rue de la Bûcherie, where you'll still find it today. It was here that a new wave of writers, including Allen Ginsberg, Anaïs Nin, and William Burroughs, gravitated in the 1950s and the great tradition of hosting "tumbleweed" guests took hold. It's now run by George's daughter, Sylvia Whitman, and has expanded to include a publishing arm, podcast, and café, but writers can still request to stay in return for helping out in the shop.

CHAPTER 9

Southern Paris

The south of Paris encompasses many neighborhoods, and for locals it would be strange to consider this part of the city as one entity. Communities run the gamut from fancy districts on the southern edges of Saint-Germain to more run down areas near the city's perimeter—but in general they're predominantly residential and mostly peaceful. You're unlikely to head south for a night out, or make a pilgrimage to the museums or galleries here, yet if you skip this part of Paris entirely you'll miss out on an authentic and less-visited side of the city. It's also an excellent place to stay if you're in search of safe, good-value places to stay that are just a short métro ride from the heart of the action.

Many people get no farther than Montparnasse. Its boulevard cafés were once an extension of Saint-Germain's bohemian scene, among them La Closerie des Lilas, frequented by everyone from Jean-Paul Sartre to Oscar Wilde, and Le Dôme, where artists including Picasso, Matisse, and Modigliani once gathered. A short walk away, the theaters and cabarets they supported still line rue de la Gaité. You can pay your respects at the Cimetière du Montparnasse, where many of the quartier's great writers, including Baudelaire and Simone de Beauvoir, were laid to rest.

For Montparnasse at its liveliest today, stroll market streets like rue Daguerre or catch an interesting contemporary art exhibition at the Jean Nouvel–designed Fondation Cartier pour l'Art Contemporain. Sadly, Montparnasse is now best known for the views from its controversial skyscraper, the Tour Montparnasse, built in 1973 to much chagrin, and the somewhat morbid Les Catacombes de Paris, filled with bones and skulls exhumed from the city's cemeteries in the 1800s.

Farther to the southeast, busy Place d'Italie is the other southern hub. Directly to the south is village-like Butte-aux-Cailles, a slice of small-town France in the capital and one of the loveliest neighborhoods for a quiet dinner or Sunday stroll when the press of the city becomes too much.

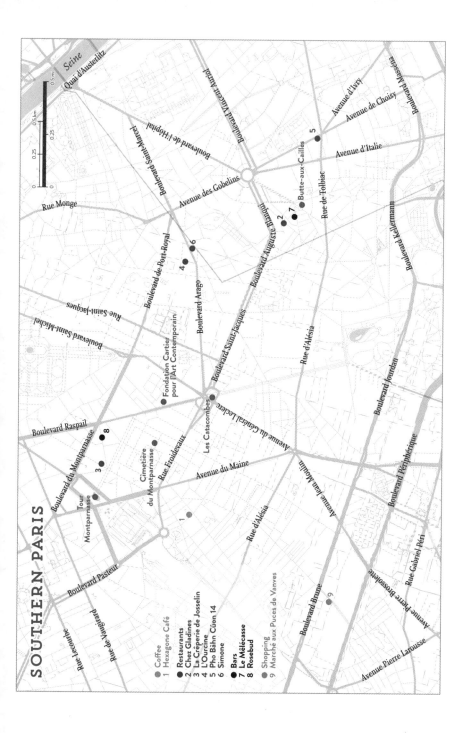

SOUTHERN PARIS

Coffee
1 Hexagone Café

Restaurants
2 Chez Gladines
3 La Crêperie de Josselin
4 L'Ourcine
5 Pho Bành Cûon 14
6 Simone

Bars
7 Le Mélécasse
8 Rosebud

Shopping
9 Marché aux Puces de Vanves

SEE

Fondation Cartier pour l'Art Contemporain

261 boulevard Raspail, 14th
Closed Monday
fondationcartier.com

Opened in 1994 and designed by celebrated architect Jean Nouvel, the Fondation Cartier pour l'Art Contemporain is among the most important modern art spaces in the city, predating both the Fondation Louis Vuitton and the Palais de Tokyo. It's an arresting building, made from steel and glass, and can even be visited independently of the gallery on Saturday tours. Inside, the focus is on exhibitions, usually two or three each year, which have included the likes of Juergen Teller's *Do you know what I mean?* and Bernie Krause's immersive *Great Animal Orchestra*. The Fondation also organizes shows abroad, taking works as far away as Buenos Aires and Seoul.

Tour Montparnasse

33 avenue du Maine, 15th
Open daily
tourmontparnasse56.com

So controversial when it was opened that it was decreed no more skyscrapers could be built in the center of Paris, the Tour Montparnasse has plenty of critics. It's a running joke that this monolith only offers the best views of the city because once you've ascended to the 56th-floor observation deck, you can't see the tower itself. If you're into panoramic vistas, hop aboard what's said to be Europe's fastest elevator to see for yourself. If you've already snapped your rooftop shots from the steps of the Sacré-Cœur, you could easily give it a miss. Exciting changes, however, are afoot. The Tour Montparnasse is set to get a complete "green" makeover in time for the 2024 Olympics, with a new rooftop conservatory and smartened-up exterior.

CLOCKWISE FROM THE TOP: RUE MOUFFETARD; BUTTE-AUX-CAILLES; EARLY EVENING IN THE 13TH ARRONDISSEMENT

Les Catacombes de Paris

1 avenue du Colonel Henri Rol-Tanguy, 14th
Closed Monday
catacombes.paris.fr

If you want to see a more macabre side to Parisian history, and aren't daunted by descending 130 steps into a labyrinth of tunnels that once formed part of a stone quarry, take a detour to the catacombs for an hour-long a tour. For around €30 (including a worthwhile queue jump), you can enter the ossuary. The remains of millions of Parisians were moved here as cemeteries were closed in the 18th and 19th centuries, among them the Cimetière des Innocents, the site of which is marked by a fountain in the Marais today. Only 1 mile of tunnels are open to the public—and don't get any ideas about wandering off the map. In 2017 two teenagers were lost underground for three days after veering out of the section open to the public.

Cimetière du Montparnasse

3 boulevard Edgar Quinet, 14th
Open daily

The Cimetière du Montparnasse is the second largest in the city after Père Lachaise, but remains much less visited. It was built on farmland in the 1800s, and you can still spot the base of a windmill amid the elaborate gravestones—numbering more than 35,000 in total with burials still taking place here today. The most famous people laid to rest here include Baudelaire, Serge Gainsbourg, Jean-Paul Sartre, and Simone de Beauvoir, as well as Pierre Larousse, the author of cookery bible *Larousse Gastronomique*. You should also seek out sculptor Constantin Brâncuși's work *Le Baiser* (The Kiss), which marks the grave of his friend and Russian anarchist Tania Rachevskaia.

Butte-aux-Cailles

13th

As Paris expanded over the centuries, what were once satellite villages became slowly incorporated into the city. Some, like Montmartre, have gradually lost their own identity. Others, including Butte-aux-Cailles, remain delightfully sleepy backwaters. Despite being just a short walk from busy Place d'Italie, this neighborhood, with its quiet cobbled streets and chilled-out bars, feels a world away from the urban landscapes that surround it. These days it's a cool spot to hang out and admire the street art that intermingles with half-timbered houses and ivy-draped street lamps. In summer you can take

BUTTE-AUX-CAILLES

a dip in the outdoor pools at Piscine de la Butte-aux-Cailles on Place Paul Verlaine. It opened in 1924 and is fed by a natural spring.

La Petite Ceinture

14th

Even in a city where space is at a premium everywhere you look, there's still a chance for a little off-grid urban exploration. The prime place to start is the Petite Ceinture, a now mostly abandoned railway line that encircles the heart of Paris. Built in the late 19th century to transport goods around the city, it closed in 1993 and mostly fell into disrepair. Intrepid souls have (not entirely legally) been staging photo shoots along its overgrown tracks for years, but it's only recently that efforts have been made to officially open more of the route. Sections totaling around 6 miles are in the process of being opened to the public as nature and heritage trails, accessed via different gateways in arrondissements ranging from the 20th to the 14th (check paris.fr/petiteceinture for the latest spots to explore).

COFFEE

Hexagone Café

121 rue du Château, 14th
Closed Monday

For a caffeine fix south of the Jardin du Luxembourg, head to Hexagone, both a roaster and coffee shop. The noisettes, cappuccinos, and filter coffees here are of great quality, and you can pick up a bag of beans to take home. The downside? Coffee is serious business, so there's no wi-fi to distract you—although you might find this provides a welcome excuse to put away your phone, order a slice of cheesecake, and watch the world go by. They also do coffees to-go if you want to pick up a frappé or a latte before a wander in the Cimetière du Montparnasse.

RESTAURANTS

Chez Gladines

30 rue des Cinq Diamants, 13th
Open daily
chezgladines-butteauxcailles.fr

If you're a fan of vexillology (the study of flags) you'll quickly guess what this restaurant is all about. The Basque flag flies proudly outside Chez Gladines, where the specialty is hearty, down-to-earth cooking from France's southwest, with mains around just €15. On plastic red-and-white check tablecloths you can tuck into dishes you may already be familiar with (goat's cheese and bacon salads, steaks, omelets) and those you may never have tried before, including *cassoulet basque* (a rich bean and sausage casserole), *pipérade* (a tomato, onion, and pepper stew), or duck breast served pink with a roquefort sauce. It's the kind of food you'll be raving about long after your trip.

La Crêperie de Josselin

67 rue du Montparnasse, 14th
Closed Monday and Tuesday

The most famous of the crêperies in Montparnasse, La Crêperie de Josselin is also one of the most traditional. If you don't have time to make the two-hour train journey from Gare Montparnasse to Brittany, this is as close to the coastline as you can get. Settle into the wood-paneled dining room for crispy-edged galettes oozing with spinach, egg, bacon, and cream, or topped with smoked salmon and lemon. Then, once your palate is cleansed with a few mouthfuls of green salad and a sip of cider, it's time for dessert: perhaps a crêpe flambéed with Grand Marnier or topped with banana, chocolate, and coconut ice cream.

L'Ourcine

92 rue Broca, 13th
Closed Sunday and Monday
restaurant-lourcine.fr

Plump scallops swimming in parsley butter on the half shell, creamy pea velouté elegantly poured into your bowl at the table, vanilla pots de crème, and spiced poached pears: L'Ourcine does classic bistro cooking so good you wonder why it once fell out of fashion. This is definitely an in-the-know spot, with French-only menus (expect to spend around €40 a head), so put away your phone and embrace the art of leisurely dining. Even though it's in a quiet residential area, it's well worth going out of your way for a meal here.

Pho Bàhn Cúon 14

129 avenue de Choisy, 13th
Open daily

Paris meets Hanoi near the Parc de Choisy, and as you sit at a street-side table covered with shiny white paper while sipping cold beer, the rest of the city starts to fade away. Obviously, there's only one thing to order here: a bowl of pho for around €15, into which you can tip chilies and bean sprouts, squirt sriracha, and rip basil until it's just to your liking. On the side get *chà giò* (deep-fried pork-stuffed rolls) which you wrap in lettuce and mint leaves, then dunk into a thin sweet chili sauce. Thanks to its quick service and reliably deep, richly flavored broth, Pho 14 is the best spot to slurp noodles around here—but beware of imitators: If it's not lit up by a red neon sign, you're in the wrong place. It's also cash only.

Simone

33 boulevard Arago, 13th
Closed Sunday and Monday
simoneparis.com

Split into a cave and restaurant, Simone does modern seasonal cooking and biodynamic wines with aplomb—somewhat of a surprise deep in the 13th arrondissement. In the evening you can discover something new with their five-dish €50 tasting menu or go à la carte. Whatever you choose will be beautifully presented. You could start with a butternut and sage soup, before miso chicken breast and girolles, or cod with fennel and lemon. At lunchtime plats are a complete steal at around €15.

BARS

Le Mêlécasse

12 rue de la Butte aux Cailles, 13th
Open daily
restaurant-melecasse.com

On a street known for small and crowded (albeit excellent) dive bars, Le Mêlécasse is the place to head when you want a bit more space—perhaps a table en terrasse with a pint of Paris-brewed IPA or an Aperol spritz and a planche de fromage. In the spirit of Butte-aux-Cailles, it's laid-back and easy going with rough stone walls and traditional wicker chairs out front. Food ranges from burgers to grilled salmon, but you could quite happily just sip cocktails until they close around 1:30 a.m.

Rosebud

11 rue Delambre, 14th
Open daily

This timeless Parisian institution was once the hangout of Simone de Beauvoir and Jean-Paul Sartre, and it still keeps the spirit of a different era alive, complete with bartenders in suits and all. More casual and affordable than golden-age cocktail bars in central Paris, it's one of the worst kept secrets of the 14th arrondissement. Although it opened in the 1960s, the vibe is more 1930s with a menu of pricey martinis and retro wonders like the Singapore Sling. Food is available, but it's really an elegant drinks spot, set to a jazz soundtrack, bien sûr.

MARCHÉ AUX PUCES DE VANVES

Marché aux Puces de Vanves

Avenue Georges Lafenestre and avenue Marc Sangnier, 14th

Saturday and Sunday 7 a.m. to 2 p.m.

Les Puces de Saint-Ouen, across the city at Paris's northerly pole, generally garners the most attention. But this scrappy flea market, way out by the Porte de Vanves in the farthest reaches of the 14th arrondissement, is where the real treasure hunters come. It's well worth the journey. On the more affordable end of the scale you'll find glassware, jewelry, vintage cameras, and the like. Just a couple of euros could bag you a set of champagne saucers or a hand luggage–sized vase. If you've got more to spend, you can get into the antiques and artwork—even taxidermy if that takes your fancy. Stalls simply set up in the road, so if the weather's poor, don't be surprised if clearing up starts early.

CHAPTER 10

Tours and Day Trips

THE CHÂTEAU DE SCEAUX

MONET'S GARDENS
AT GIVERNY

Paris is a fascinating and complex city. You could spend years learning about its history and culture—and many people do. So how do you get a feel for the French capital in just a few days? The easiest option is to fast-track your cultural immersion and take a tour to get under the skin of the city. Options are myriad, ranging from culinary experiences led by industry experts in food and wine to movie-themed romps in the footsteps of *Midnight in Paris* or *Julie & Julia*. Small group tour companies abound, so there's no reason to resort to an open-top bus tour or a "follow-the-umbrella" group excursion.

If you can tear yourself away from the center of Paris, there are also a slew of fantastic day trips on the city's doorstep that will give you more of an insight into France. As in many capitals, life in Paris moves at a different pace to the rest of the country. Far-reaching RER connections and speedy regional trains make it a breeze to explore, so you're usually best off arranging your own travel—otherwise you'll find yourself with a hefty limo bill or in the midst of overbooked coach tours.

Many Parisians own, or dream of owning, a home outside the city and you'll be in the company of plenty of locals if you join the weekend exodus. Once you clear the *banlieues* (suburbs), you'll discover that Paris is surrounded by rolling countryside dotted by majestic castles and historic towns. With an overnight stay you can visit the neatly manicured vineyards of Champagne, while the rural Normandy landscapes that inspired Monet are barely an hour away. For historical significance, it's hard to match the drama of the grand palaces of Versailles and Fontainebleau. Both were at one time royal residences and still have the opulence to match. Lesser-known châteaux on a slightly more manageable scale include Sceaux on the city's southern fringes, mostly visited for its glorious gardens, and Chantilly, known for its associations with the improbable combination of horse racing and whipped cream.

TOURS IN THE CITY

Paris by Mouth

parisbymouth.com

If you really want to get to grips with French food culture, the exceptional small group tours led by Paris by Mouth are the perfect place to start. Their three-hour experiences mix sit-down tastings with walks around the Marais, Saint-Germain, or the Latin Quarter. They're pricey at over €100 a head but offer unrivaled insight, picking up raves from the likes of the *New York Times* and *Travel + Leisure*. Spend a morning with one of their knowledgeable experts and you could find yourself becoming acquainted with the art of charcuterie, getting an insider's guide to finding the best produce at a local market, or learning what really makes a perfect croissant.

Set in Paris

setinparis.com

Run by Abigail de Bruyne, a British-American who now calls Paris home, Set in Paris are movie buffs extraordinaire. You can dip your toe into silver-screen history on one of their affordable walking tours, tracing the locations of blockbusters such as *The Hunchback of Notre-Dame*, *Julie & Julia*, *The Devil Wears Prada*, and *The Bourne Identity*, or focus on the spots made famous by classics such as *Amélie* or *Midnight in Paris*. They also offer a couple of options not inspired by the big screen, including an excellent introduction to Coco Chanel's Paris including hot chocolate at her favorite café, Angelina, and an informative stroll along rue Saint-Honoré.

Cedric's Paris

cedricsparis.com

Touring Paris in a vintage Citroën 2CV is an experience you'll never forget—and one that'll leave you with an envy-inducing set of vacation photos. Produced from 1948 to 1990, the car is an icon of French design, created to carry four people and 100 pounds of potatoes at a maximum speed of 40 miles an hour. Various hotels and private operators have realized that these little workhorses look rather picturesque in modern-day Paris, but boutique tour company Cedric's Paris continue to rack up the best reviews. They offer day and night tours as well as curated photographer-led photo shoots for newlyweds and honeymooners. Their four cars (named Thelma, Juliette, Yuna, and Louise) can be booked individually for up to three people or as a group.

Context Travel

contexttravel.com

Context might be a major operator, offering private guides and small-group tours worldwide, but they remain one of the best choices for the intellectually curious. You can join them for food and wine experiences or general city introductions, but they really come into their own if your interests are more specialized. Book in for a three-hour deep dive into the history of the French Revolution, discover Hemingway's Paris, or learn more about how jazz came to flourish in the city of lights. Guides are usually educated to MA or PhD level in their areas of expertise.

Château de Versailles

You simply can't come to Paris and not make time for at least a half-day trip to Versailles, Louis XIV's astonishingly extravagant palace and sprawling formal gardens. He continued work started by his father, Louis XIII, transforming a royal hunting lodge into Europe's most lavish residence, which would become the seat of the French court in 1682. Its excess is hard to comprehend. All in all, it took more than 30,000 craftsmen and laborers to bring Louis XIV's vision to life. The palace holds 2,300 rooms, and the gardens feature 400 sculptures and 1,400 fountains.

No matter what time you arrive, you'll almost always have to wait in line to enter the palace. The trick to escaping the crowds is to tackle the most famous rooms first, before visitor numbers build. This means that the glitzy State Apartments should be top of your itinerary—this is where Louis XIV's excesses are most evident. Most magical is the Hall of Mirrors, lavishly decorated by Jules Hardouin-Mansart with chandeliers, frescos, and gold statuary. It's still used for the rare state occasion: Comparatively recent visitors have included Queen Elizabeth and the Kennedys.

Along with all Versailles's luxury came strict rules governing life at court. The Mesdames' Apartments offer more human insight, tracing the lives of Adélaïde and Victoire, daughters of Louis XIV's successor, Louis XV. Pick up an audio guide to learn about the intrusive public waking and sleeping ceremonies that they were subjected to throughout their lives at court.

André Le Nôtre's sprawling formal gardens, mixing peaceful groves with grand topiary-lined avenues, offer the breath of fresh air you'll need by the time you've taken in the palace's main rooms. The Orangerie, covered with orange and palm trees in summer, is particularly impressive. Farther out is the Grand Canal, where you can hire row boats in summer. On the grounds you'll also find two smaller palaces, missed by many visitors. The Grand Trianon, surrounded by pink marble colonnades, was built by Louis XIV for his mistress, Madame de Montespan; the Petit Trianon was Marie Antoinette's wedding gift from her new husband, Louis XVI. It's said that husband and wife never spent the night here; instead this is where "Madame Déficit" threw her lavish parties. Marie Antoinette also built a fascinating faux Normandy-style hamlet in the grounds of her personal château, complete with a working farm still in use and open to visitors today.

INSIDER TIP: Skip the overpriced cafés in the palace grounds and venture into the town of Versailles itself for lunch or dinner. There's an outdoor market in the Place du Marché Notre-Dame on Tuesday, Friday, and Sunday mornings, and there's plenty of choices when it comes to restaurants. For lunch, try La Mangette (38 rue Carnot), a sweet little place that does salads, soups, and delicious desserts to eat in and take out in smart cardboard boxes.

PRACTICALITIES:

▶ Despite the abundance of organized tours to Versailles, you really don't need a coach and a guide to get the most from a visit. Getting here is easy: Hop on the RER C to Versailles Château–Rive Gauche. It's a 10-minute walk from the station to the palace.

▶ The best value ticket to visit the palace is the €20 "passport," which includes access to the Grand Trianon, Petit Trianon, and the Domaine de Marie Antoinette. You can visit the gardens for free.

Monet's Gardens at Giverny

If you were mesmerized by *Les Nymphéas* at the Musée de l'Orangerie and want to learn more about the artist who painted them, Monet's rural home in the village of Giverny is an easy day trip from the city. He lived in Normandy from 1883 until his death in 1926 and was endlessly inspired by its bucolic landscapes. Not only did he work on his famous water lily series here but also a sequence of 20 or so haystack paintings that first led him to approach the same subject across different seasons, weather conditions, and times of day.

Surrounded by peaceful countryside, Giverny has changed little since Monet's day. Although the stone cottages seem to be completely given over to celebrating the artist's life, or turned into contemporary studios and boutiques, the town remains utterly charming.

The Fondation Claude Monet has sensitively preserved Monet's house and gardens just as when he lived and worked here. While the water lilies only bloom in July and August, Monet planted his garden to be enjoyed throughout the year—so whenever you come, you won't be disappointed. A team of gardeners attentively tends to the grounds, and strict ticketing keeps the crowds manageable.

Start in the Clos Normand, the classical garden that runs down the gentle slope from the house. This was the first garden Monet designed, a romantic mix of rose-draped arches and narrow nasturtium-carpeted pathways. To the untrained eye it looks almost wild in places, but it's actually meticulously organized to give the perfect combinations of color and symmetry throughout the seasons. Monet didn't purchase the land that would become his famous Japanese-inspired Water Garden until 10 years after his arrival in Giverny. It was once across a railroad track, but now it's split from the Clos Normand by a road and accessed through a tunnel. It's a complete contrast. Instead of flowerbeds and fruit trees, here you'll find winding streams, ponds, and walkways shaded by soaring bamboo. Like all the Impressionists, Monet advocated plein air painting, and it was beneath the Water Garden's weeping willows he sat outdoors capturing the water lilies that would become the subject of his most renowned work.

Don't leave without a quick tour of Monet's house. It's surprisingly modest and homely, its dusky pink exterior offset by chrome green shutters. Inside, his bold use of color extends to the yellow dining room and a petit salon bleu, filled with prints by Japanese artist Kitagawa Utamaro. If you have time, you could also stop at the one modern addition to Giverny: the Musée des Impressionnismes, which hosts small but interesting exhibitions linked to the Impressionist movement.

INSIDER TIP: If you're ready for a workout, it's most fun to make your own way to Giverny. Hop on a train from Gare Saint-Lazare to the nearby town of Vernon, which takes around 45 minutes, then hire bikes from the café opposite Vernon station. It's a half-hour cycle to Giverny, mostly along paths rather than roads, and the café will give you a map.

PRACTICALITIES:

▶ The house and gardens are open from late March to the end of November, but exact dates change each year. Book tickets online for a shorter wait on the day you visit.

▶ If you don't cycle or take an organized trip from Paris, there's a shuttle bus from Vernon to the gardens.

Parc de Sceaux

As well as the sprawling châteaux grounds at Versailles, there are other delightful gardens closer to the city, including those at Parc de Sceaux (pronounced "so"). Despite being designed by André Le Nôtre, the same landscape architect behind Versailles's grand avenues, this enormous park remains one of the city's best-kept secrets.

If you're in search of symmetry, topiary, and fountains, start in the formal gardens falling gracefully away from the château down a gentle slope, an oval pool at their center. From here it's interesting to wander between the buildings that were once integral to the running of the domaine: the orangery, designed by Jules Hardouin-Mansart and now used to house the estate's statuary, and the pretty Petit Château, a mansion originally built as a guesthouse in the 1600s.

Beyond, there are more than 180 hectares to explore, so the park never feels crowded. Things get wilder as you follow Sceaux's Grand Canal to the Plaine de la Patte d'Oie, where there are grassy banks to relax on. Running parallel are the Cascades, an impressive series of stone-built waterfalls that culminate in the fountain-filled Octagone pool. If you've come to picnic or see the cherry blossom in spring, head to the woody Bosquet Nord where the trees usually bloom from April. Nearby is the unexpected but poignant Mémorial de la Déportation des Juifs des Hauts-de-Seine, cast-iron statues depicting the 12 tribes of Israel in memory of the region's holocaust victims.

The Château de Sceaux, however, is a grand country house rather than a palace. Although it looks impressive from the outside, it was rebuilt after the revolution in 1830s, making it relatively modern by French standards. Filled with traditional displays of art, porcelain, and furniture, it isn't really worth a visit unless you want to delve deeper into Sceaux's history. It's only open in the afternoon and is closed on Mondays.

INSIDER TIP: Most Parisians come to Sceaux for one reason only: to picnic in the gardens in the spring and summer. You could bring supplies with you, but it's more fun to shop in the town of Sceaux itself. You can pick up fantastic baguettes, cheeses, terrines, and the like on pedestrianized rue Houdan on your way to the park, or you can stop by the local market on Wednesday or Saturday mornings.

PRACTICALITIES:

▶ The park is open year round, but it's renowned as one of the best spots in Paris to see the cherry blossom. In June, there are usually a couple of nights of open-air opera.

▶ If you want to go straight to the park, take the RER B to Parc de Sceaux. If you want to stop by a boulangerie first, take the branch to Sceaux. Either journey is about 30 minutes from the centre of Paris.

Champagne

Inscribed on the UNESCO World Heritage List in 2015 for its outstanding cultural significance, Champagne might be the world's most prestigious wine region. It's also one of the easiest to visit. The center of production is the bucolic countryside surrounding the small city of Reims, where great houses such Ruinart, Veuve Clicquot, Mumm, and Taittinger welcome visitors for tours and tastings. With the train from Paris taking just 45 minutes, you can easily visit in a day. But you might consider staying overnight if you want to take tours into the vineyards, see Reims's magnificent cathedral, or explore the town of Épernay, considered the capital of the wine region.

In Europe, only sparkling wine made here can be legally sold as Champagne, and a strict set of rules and regulations control productions. Only the grapes Chardonnay, Pinot Meunier, and Pinot Noir may be used with every bottle that is at least three years in the making. Champagne is first fermented as a still white wine before being blended and undergoing a secondary fermentation in bottle for at least 15 months, although many cellars opt for much longer. This means each house has their own distinctive style—and you can't beat tasting your way through their collections on location.

Cellar visits in Reims should be booked at least a week in advance and start at round €20. Taittinger and Mumm are the easiest to visit, with English tours that can be reserved online. Tattinger's cellars (still family owned) are simply magnificent, occupying the *caves* of the now destroyed Abbaye Saint-Nicaise, which are partly built into a Roman quarry. Mumm's tours are more informative, so you can easily combine both in a day without feeling like you're hearing the same stories twice. The number of bottles stored beneath the city is simply astonishing: mile-upon-mile of cellars stretch beneath the city.

INSIDER TIP: All tours of major houses include a tasting, but if you want to try the really interesting bottles that don't get exported, head to Trésors de Champagne. This boutique and tasting room specializes in small-scale and grower champagnes that you can try by the glass or tasting flights. The English-speaking staff will offer plenty of insights along the way.

PRACTICALITIES:

▶ If you want to visit the more prestigious houses, be prepared to reserve weeks in advance and pay up to €80. Trips into the vineyards can also be pricey and vary widely in quality—check with the tourist office for their recommendations.

▶ Reims has two stations: the Gare de Reims is in the center of town and walking distance from most cellars; the Gare de Champagne-Ardenne TGV is a 20 minute cab ride out of town.

CHAPTER 11

Survival Guide

CLOCKWISE FROM TOP LEFT: A TRADITIONAL PARISIAN BOULANGERIE; MARKET DAY; A QUIET WEEKEND IN THE 9TH; THE PARIS MÉTRO

Paris is an easy city to fall in love with, and you certainly don't need a survival guide for a three-day trip. But if you want to delve a little deeper into French culture, then learning more about local etiquette is a good place to start. The only challenges you're really likely to face exploring Paris are practical: how to navigate the métro, place an order in a restaurant, or get to the airport. Plus the city—like all other big capitals—has its little idiosyncrasies, from shops that frustratingly close without warning on Mondays to local slang that throws you off even when you're *sure* you've just mastered the language.

CULTURE

Etiquette

Parisians have an entirely unwarranted reputation as being cold and aloof. Often you just need to make a little effort to break the ice. A simple "bonjour" or "merci" in your best French accent will go a long way in shops and restaurants, as will wishing someone a *bonne journée* (a good day) or *bonne soirée* (good evening) as you leave. When you become more familiar with the language, you should be careful to only address people you know well with the pronoun "tu." Strictly, you should always use "vous" when you first meet someone, until you're invited to do otherwise. If you get to know someone well, embrace the custom of *la bise* (two cheek-to-cheek air kisses used as a greeting and farewell between friends—but certainly not strangers).

Otherwise, the usual rules of being a traveler in a new country apply. Be mindful when taking photos in busy places, and ask for permission before you photograph others. Take note that people may talk more quietly than you're used to, and that loud, raucous tables will not be welcome in some restaurants. You may also need to bear with getting pushed around a little more than you're used to at home, whether queuing for your morning croissant or getting on the métro.

Food and Drink

Entire books have been written on French dining etiquette. Food is central to the country's culture, and tradition can dictate how dishes are cooked, how they're served, and how you should eat them. Dining is often a form of theater. The flourish of a final flambé, the uncorking of a bottle of wine, and the tap on the crust of a crème brûlée are not just culinary but sensory experiences. The ritual of a French gourmet meal is so sacred, it's even inscribed on the UNESCO World Heritage List. Do you need to follow all the rules to eat well? No. But following a few guidelines can will help you along the way.

First things first, consider where you're eating. If it's a restaurant, call ahead to make a reservation, or try your luck and ask if they have space and wait to be seated. By contrast, in cafés and on terrasses you generally seat yourself then wait to be spotted by a waiter who'll ask for your order. It's very bad form to make a reservation and not show up.

Most meals follow a set format. A basket of bread generally arrives (without butter) as soon as you've ordered. You can snack on this before your food arrives, or use it to mop up sauce on your plate during your meal. It's totally acceptable to place a piece of baguette on the table in-between tearing off pieces; you'll rarely be given a plate. To follow, anything between one and three courses is the norm. Often restaurants offer two set formules: *entrée-plat-dessert* (starter, main, and dessert), an *entrée-plat* (starter and main), or a *plat-dessert* (main and dessert). Note that "entrée" means appetizer, not main course. Unless you're eating soup, it's polite to use both a knife and fork, never just a fork or spoon in your right hand. Dishes will only be cleared once everyone at the table has finished.

When it comes to drinks, the carafe is your friend. It's normal to eschew pricey bottled water for *une carafe d'eau* (a jug of tap water); and many restaurants will also serve wine by the 250ml or 500ml carafe—ideal if you're not up to putting away a full bottle at lunch. After your meal, if you order *un café*, you'll get a bitter espresso with a packet of sugar on the side. For an Americano (espresso lengthened with hot water) ask for a *café allongé*. *Un café américain* or *un café filtre* will usually get you a filter coffee. If you want hot milk added, it's *un café au lait*. Frothy lattes are hard to find outside specialty coffee shops, but there are two uniquely French options to try: the *café crème* (espresso topped with steamed milk, close to a cappuccino but slightly less foamy) and the *café noisette* (espresso with the tiniest splash of milk so it's the color of a *noisette,* or hazelnut).

HOW TO ORDER A STEAK

The most frequent restaurant dilemma in France is how to order steak. From duck to lamb, red meats are generally served pink. Unless you specify a preference, steaks may come bloodier than you might expect. Here's how to request your preferred cuisson.

Bleu: Quickly seared on the outside and nearly raw in the middle.

Saignant: Literally meaning bloody, this is the equivalent of rare.

À point: Medium to medium-rare, usually still a little pink.

Bien cuit: Well done and cooked through.

Très bien cuit: Very well done, an order likely to result in raised eyebrows.

Steak tartare, of course, is something else entirely. This delicious but (for some) daunting dish of chopped raw steak is entirely uncooked and traditionally topped with a raw egg yolk. Every restaurant has their own take on the recipe, varying how finely the meat is chopped and the balance of seasonings. Accoutrements usually include finely minced shallots, capers, gherkins, and parsley, plus splashes of Worcestershire sauce and Tabasco. Sometimes you can mix your own at the table.

As for getting the check, you'll need to ask for it—bills aren't provided unless they're requested. Never, ever, call over a waiter by shouting, "Garçon!" Catch their eye with a nod of your head, then ask for "l'addition, s'il vous plaît." Doggy bags and to-go boxes are unheard of: It's expected that you'll finish all the food on your plate, and if you don't, you certainly can't take away your leftovers—so wave goodbye to that slice of *tarte tatin* that would have been just delicious for breakfast.

Tipping 101

Tipping in France isn't always straightforward. Restaurant bills are traditionally meant to be inclusive of service, but it's customary to usually leave a little extra. Locals might tip anywhere from a few euros to 10 percent—although some resolutely leave nothing at all. If you do decide to tip, note that tips are not added to card payments, so keep some spare cash handy. For a coffee, a few small coins will suffice. Taxis and Ubers will always appreciate a tip, but it's not expected.

Language

Parisians can speak incredibly fast, and it takes a while to get tuned in to their pace. The city is also rife with slang it would take years to learn. Regularly thrown around phrases like *c'est pas mal* (it's not bad) actually mean the opposite of what you think—in this case, with the right intonation, that something's great. Then there's the slang called verlan, which is becoming ever more incorporated into general usage. It's essentially a reversal of syllables. For example: *fou* (crazy) becomes *ouf*; *lourd* (heavy) is twisted to *relou* (meaning boring); and you might not throw a *fête* (party) but a *teuf*. You also might hear the terms *mec* (guy) and *meuf* (woman), although the latter is often derogatory.

So where should you start? Simply with a handy app, ideally one with offline live translation, like Google Translate. Using it, you can point your phone camera at a menu and read it in English without even having to type.

Apéro: A predinner drink that often extends long into the evening.

Briquet: A lighter, which you're likely to be asked for frequently if you're en terrasse.

Ça marche: Literally meaning "it works" but used like "sure, great" to indicate agreement.

Un démi: A half pint of beer, an ideal *apéro* order.

Été?: The past tense of *être*, the verb meaning "to be." You'll hear it regularly in the question, "*Ça a été?*" (how was it?), asked by waiters at the end of a meal.

Fermé: Closed. How you will find many shops and restaurants on Sundays and Mondays.

Grève: Hopefully you won't encounter a *grève*, or strike, during your trip—but they're a common occurrence, particularly among transportation workers.

Haut de gamme: Upscale or high end, a term that applies to many of the city's *grands magasins* (large department stores) and boutiques.

Île-de-France: Not France, as you could assume, but the wider Parisian region. It's a useful term to know when you're buying métro tickets. A standard T+ ticket will only cover you in the center of Paris; you'll need an IDF (Île-de-France) point-to-point ticket if you want to travel farther.

Joie de vivre: Simply "the joy of living," one of the greatest French concepts.

Kiffer: A slang verb meaning to love something. For instance, "*Je kiffe ça*" (I love that).

Lèche-vitrines: While this phrase translates to "licking windows," it actually means window shopping.

Métro: Loved and hated by locals in equal measure, the Paris métro is for better or worse a symbol of the city.

Non: The French are renowned for calling things how they see them, and they have an often-blunt approach to tackling sensitive topics. *Non*, or "no," is a word that's likely to come in handy.

Ouf: The verlan for fou, often used to imply that something is crazy or mad.

Putain: Parisians' currently favored swear word, the French equivalent of "fuck."

Quoi: Meaning "what," quoi can be used as a statement to express confusion (*quoi?*), and in the most lovely of French sayings, "Je ne sais quoi," it describes that indefinable quality that can't be expressed in words.

Rendezvous: A meeting (often shortened to "rdv") rather than a romantic encounter, as you might imagine when the word is used in English.

Sympa: Meaning "cool" or "good," sympa can be used to talk about something or someone.

Tak: *Tak*, or more often *tak tak tak*, is almost untranslatable, more a sound than a word. You'll hear it muttered plenty, like when someone is checking things off a list.

Utile: Simply translated as "useful," *utile* is a word key to Parisian life. Canvas shopping bags? Utile. Plenty of cash? Utile.

Vélib's: The gray bikes that you can hire for free across the city.

Wi-fi: Pronounced "wee-fee," for which you'll need the *mot de passe* (password).

X: Very few French words begin with the letter "x," and if you think you hear someone say it, they're probably talking about "Aix," a town in Provence pronounced as the letter in English.

Yaourt: There's no simpler way to start your day than with a pot of unsweetened *yaourt* (yogurt), which is a staple in homes and on hotel buffets.

Zéro: Easy to guess, *zéro* means "zero." Use it to order a glass of on-trend *zéro dosage* champagne, a style drier than a classic brut.

The gameified language-learning app Duolingo is the best option to brush up on the basics before your trip. Don't worry if you don't get that far. If you make a little effort in French, you'll find people are more than happy to help you out—and most will speak some English. You're very unlikely to find yourself in a situation without an English speaker at least somewhere nearby.

TRANSPORT

Mastering the Métro

Paris is an easy city to get around. If you don't decide to walk absolutely everywhere, you'll find the métro the most useful. Start by buying a *carnet,* 10 single-journey métro and bus tickets that you can pick up from a machines at most métro stops for around €15 (touch-screen terminals usually have an English option). Next, throw away any paper maps you have and download Citymapper. It will calculate any journey, right down to the best exit to take from the métro, and keep you updated with live delays.

Entering the métro itself, your ticket will be spat back out at the first set of automatic barriers. Don't discard it: Random checks, although rare, require you to present a valid ticket on request. To exit the métro, you just push through a set of stiff swinging doors. The only exception is when you're changing lines somewhere tricky, like in the bowels of Châtelet-Les Halles, Europe's largest métro interchange, when you may find yourself needing to re-present your ticket through an unexpected entry gate en route.

International Connections

By plane, you're likely to arrive outside of the city at Charles de Gaulle Airport (CDG) or Orly. The former has the easiest connections to the city center—a short journey on the RER B, one of the rapid transit lines that extend beyond the core métro routes. From Orly, to the south, it's a slightly longer journey with a short hop on the Orlyval shuttle train before you connect with the RER B at Antony. Both public transport connections will cost you around €10–15 one-way and take half an hour or so. Taxis will be upward of €50 and aren't really worth it unless you're in a group. Budget bus links might be cheap, but they're slow and irregular.

Book ahead and you can also easily travel to other European capitals by train. Eurostar links Gare du Nord with London St Pancras in just 2 hours 17 minutes via the Channel Tunnel, while Thalys trains run direct from Gare du Nord to Brussels (1 hour 30 minutes) and Amsterdam (3 hours 20 minutes). You can even be whisked from Gare de Lyon to various Swiss destinations in 3 to 4 hours, Barcelona in a little over 6 hours, and Milan or Turin in 8 hours. Seat61.com is the best resource for planning your route.

Traveling by Train Within France

High-speed TGV lines make traveling within France a breeze: They're efficient, comfortable, and generally on time. From Paris, you could hop aboard for a night away in Champagne, Lyon, or Bordeaux. You'll get the best value tickets if you book in advance, and you'll need to make a seat reservation if you're using a rail pass. You may also find local routes useful for getting to sights just outside the city center, perhaps Monet's gardens at Giverny or the Château de Chantilly. You can buy tickets for these trains on the day from touch-screen machines at the station.

Wherever you're going, there are two things to check. First, that you've got the correct station in Paris. The city has seven major rail stations, each serving different destinations. Second, remember that *compostage est obligatoire*. This means it's obligatory to *composter* (validate) a paper ticket before getting on board. Simply insert it into a small machine on the platform and it will be stamped.

Top Tips for Taxis

As in most of Europe, Uber now reigns supreme in Paris—and as in many other cities, there's friction between Uber drivers and established official taxis who feel they're being undermined. Both Uber and the taxis parisiens are fine to use. Uber is usually more convenient unless you're near a taxi rank, and often cheaper unless surge fares apply. Driver-supplied extras like USB chargers and water aren't yet widespread, but they are becoming more common. Just note that if you take Uber, while you'll use your existing account, the bank charges will be in Euros and you may incur foreign transaction fees.

DAY-TO-DAY DILEMMAS

Mondays and Sundays

Many Parisian bars and restaurants close on Sundays and Mondays, while shops can shut their doors mid-afternoon. The only way to tackle this is with a bit of advance planning. If you've got your heart set on a restaurant, double-check in advance that it will be open. You should also carefully pick the areas of the city you choose to explore: The Marais, traditionally the city's Jewish quarter, thrives on Sundays, for example.

Managing Your Cash

A few spots in Paris are still cash only, including all the city's markets, but that doesn't mean vendors will accept the crisp €50 note you're thrusting at them. Large notes present a problem: Supermarket cashiers often simply refuse to accept them, and waiters will cast their most scathing stare if you present one for a €2 coffee. Other than going to the bank, one of the more practical solutions is to pop into a supermarket like Monoprix when you need a bottle of water or some gum, and use the automatic checkout machines—they'll always give you change, no questions asked.

Chain Stores

Speaking of supermarkets, if you're self-catering it's worth becoming familiar with some Parisian brands. Of the supermarkets, Monoprix is the most upmarket, with smart homewares and specialist foods nice enough to take home as gifts. Franprix and Carrefour are cheaper, while Bio c' Bon is pick of the bunch for organic produce and fresh vegetables.

Generally, Paris is a city that prides itself on its superb range of independent retailers—but there are also a couple of useful chains to add to your mental map. Maison Landemaine, which has branches across the city, should be your go-to for pâtisserie if you find yourself in an éclair desert, while Éric Kayser's boulangeries have a solid reputation for bread. If you're craving a burger, check out the growing mini-group PNY (short for Paris-New York) before you resort to the golden arches of MacDo.

Safety

In general, Paris is a safe city. Violent crime is rare and you should feel comfortable walking the streets in the city center, even after dark, although the métro can get a bit sketchy after midnight. Outside the périphérique, the city has long battled social problems stemming from the division between the manicured center of Paris and the towering apartment blocks in some banlieues. It's true that some suburbs have high levels of deprivation and unemployment—but they are also highly stigmatized. Every few months stories surface in the international press about the latest banlieue to turn into a sharia-run no-go zone: These accounts simply aren't true and only add to the prejudice and injustice faced by these communities. Don't buy into the scaremongering.

The only things you should watch out for are pickpockets and scammers, especially in touristy areas. Carry a bag with a secure zip or closure, be wary of anyone who tries to distract you, and steer clear of the so-called "string men" who'll tie a cheap bracelet on your wrist before you've had a chance to protest and then demand an exorbitant sum.

For women, it's a great city for traveling alone. Street harassment is less frequent than in many European capitals, and thanks to the bistronomy movement, solo bar dining is becoming ever more popular. Plenty of locals regularly stop for a coffee on their own, and you certainly won't raise eyebrows if you choose to sip a glass of wine toute seule. One of the consequences of tiny Parisian apartments is that people are much more inclined to spend time in their local bars and cafés, whether to eat, to drink, or simply to read in the sunshine with a coffee.

Emergency Numbers

There's currently no equivalent to 911 or 999 in France, although debate rages around whether the country should adopt one emergency number. At the time of writing you should dial:

▶ 15 for emergency medical assistance
▶ 17 for the police
▶ 18 for the fire department

You can also call the Europe-wide emergency number 112, which will redirect you to one of the above.

CHAPTER 12

Accommodation

Whatever your hotel fantasy, you'll be able to fulfill it in Paris. This is the city of romantic rooftop vistas, winding staircases, and candle-lit cocktail bars. In every arrondissement you'll find addresses once frequented by golden-age film stars and great writers, and luxury still knows no bounds in the grandes dames of the city's hotel scene. On the other end of the spectrum are boutique hotels. Competition is fierce among them—great design is becoming de rigueur, even on a budget, and independently owned outfits are making a splash alongside international hotel groups. Space might be at a premium, but hotels are getting increasingly savvy about making the most of it, from floating boatels on the Seine to hotels that use tech to pack in hundreds of beds and still create an intimate atmosphere.

As for where to stay, unless you have your heart set on Saint-Germain or want to get a taste of local life in outer quartiers such as Belleville, it's best to opt for somewhere on the Right Bank close to the center of the city. Eiffel Tower views might be tempting, but you'll find yourself far from the heart of the action. Choosing a hotel around the Grands Boulevards and the Marais, or on the edges of Montmartre, will put you plumb in the center of all the sights, near a wide array of excellent restaurants, and in walking distance of myriad transport links. If bars, nightlife, and neo-bistros are top of your list, go a little farther east toward to the Canal Saint-Martin and Bastille.

The hotels selected here are classified into three groups. Budget are €150 a night and under, boutique fall between €150 and €250 a night, and blow-the-budget accomodations offer something really special for nights when money is no object. Of course, promotions and high-season demand can often push rates from one category into another, so check online before you book. Many hotels will offer the best deal to those who book direct.

Cool flashpacking chains with bars and rooftop terraces dominate the city's hostels. Expect to pay around €30 for a dorm bed. You'll pay much more for a private room, and it's rarely a good value unless you want to be at the heart of the backpacking party scene.

HOTEL PARIS VOLTAIRE

Renting an apartment is one of the best ways to really get a feel for Paris—and if you're on a budget, you can usually find a great one-bedroom place for around €80 a night. Spend a little more and you could find yourself staying in an elegant antique-filled home with wrought iron balconies or an artist-designed loft complete with soaring ceilings and Seine views. The other big benefit of choosing an Airbnb is that you can get a feel for a more local neighborhood: You can shop at the closest market, pick up bottles of wine and baguettes, and start to understand a few of the quirks that make Parisian life so enchanting—if occasionally frustrating. With the latter in mind, here are a few things to look out for before you book.

Check for elevators: There are many advantages to staying in a lovely historic building, though an elevator may not be one of them. Sixth or seventh floor apartments are often accessed via tightly winding staircases. Where there is an elevator, it may be tiny, just large enough for one person and a suitcase. If you're traveling with lots of luggage, double check with your host so you don't get a last-minute surprise.

Set your size expectations: Space is at a premium in Paris and generally apartments are small, with studios starting at around 12 square meters (40 square feet). In the smallest, beds are likely to be foldout futons and bathrooms may be separated by sliding doors.

Pay attention to wording: If you're translating Franglais apartment descriptions, there are a couple of words to look out for. "Refait à neuf" means refurbished, usually freshly painted with new furniture and fittings. Some cheaper apartments may sell themselves as a *nid* (nest) or *cocoon* (coccoon); see the point above and expect to get cozy.

Find your way: Parisian apartment blocks may be organized differently to what you're used to back home. Most have a large door onto the street, accessed via key code or buzzers labeled by surname. Once inside, there's a courtyard or lobby from where one or several staircases ascend to individual apartments. These are unlikely to be numbered, so you may be told to go to the "third on the left" or to look out for a distinguishing doorknocker.

Understand the kitchen: Parisian kitchens are small and functional. Fridges are often small, freezers have space for an ice tray or two, and you're likely to have just a couple of gas or electric rings to cook on. For a few days, you're unlikely to need any more.

Befriend the neighbors: As in many European cities, Airbnb is controversial in Paris. Beyond the effect of driving up property prices, short-term rentals can change the daily life of a community. In Paris, the buildings are old, the walls are thin, space is tight, and noise travels. As such, people tend to be respectful of their neighbors, and you'd be wise to behave as though you, too, were a long-term resident. That means keeping noise to a minimum late at night or even helping others up the stairs with their shopping. It goes without saying that loud, unruly visitors will not be warmly welcomed.

HOSTELS

St Christopher's Inn

Best for party lovers

5 rue de Dunkerque, 10th

st-christophers.co.uk

A mega-hostel with a heart, St Christopher's wins points for its location (one of two in Paris) near the Canal Saint-Martin and just by Gare de l'Est and Gare du Nord. It's not the most salubrious part of town, but it is incredibly convenient. Its other selling point is its enormous bar, where discounts and happy hours keep the party going every night of the week. There are also pub crawls to join and a laundry room for longer-term travelers. Dorms themselves are modern and slick, with curtained-off bunks that have individual lights, power sockets, and storage. The number of beds per room varies: some have four beds, the largest squeeze in ten.

Generator

Best for chilled-out flashpackers
9–11 place du Colonel Fabien, 10th
generatorhostels.com

This self-proclaimed designer hostel—part of a growing international chain spanning from Miami to Madrid—takes hostel accomodations to new heights. Its industrial feel is softened by colorful furniture and surprisingly fluffy beds. The rooms are all modern and neutral, giving them a relaxing feel, and are kitted out with wi-fi, full-length mirrors, USB charging points, and often en-suite bathrooms. If you book early, doubles and twins can also be decent value if you don't mind sharing a shower. Generator's crowning glory is the rooftop bar, open every afternoon and evening, and there's even Le Club in the basement if you want to stay up late.

BUDGET

Hôtel Paris Voltaire

Best for old-school simplicity
79 rue Sedaine, 11th
hotel-paris-voltaire.fr

This two-star hotel comes from a different era—one unfamiliar with charging docks and social media—but unlike some of its peers it's reliably clean and welcoming. It's also in a superb location on a quiet street. You'll be just a few minutes' walk from the best restaurants in the 11th and not much farther from the Marais. The tiny yet delightfully quirky lobby is stuffed with curios (lace-covered antique tables, leather sofas with zebra-print cushions, embroidered wall-hangings), but the rooms themselves are basic. You might find your en-suite has a turquoise-blue bath or that your walls are painted in an unusual baby-pink hue; no room is the same. There are sweet personal touches, too, like the wi-fi code handwritten on a mini chalkboard on each desk. You won't find a bar to relax at in the evening, or hotel-sponsored opportunities to meet other travelers, but if you're looking for a quiet, comfortable, and safe place to stay it's one of the city's cheapest options.

Mama Shelter

Best for bragging rights
109 rue de Bagnolet, 20th
mamashelter.com

The Parisian outpost of the Mama Shelter chain is just as hip as its siblings in LA, Prague, and Rio. Rooftop lounge loved by locals? Check. Chalkboard walls? Check. Buzzing pizza joint? Check. This is a brand whose design-led approach is so loved that they've even launched a line of merch: You can pick up a "Mama loves you" tee or one of their signature Looney Tunes–style masks at reception. The Paris location might be a little out of the city center, but you sure won't be left out of the party if you stay here. The only surprise is that the Philippe Starck–designed rooms are so affordable if you book early. All have iMacs and super-fast free wi-fi (the perfect setup for AirPlay movie sessions), a well-stocked minibar, and high-quality comfy bedding. The price varies depending on how much space you need: Small rooms sell out early for less than €100 while you can pay over double that for an XXL family suite.

citizenM Gare de Lyon

Best for high-tech comfort

8 rue Van Gogh, 12th

citizenm.com

The pod-like rooms at citizenM might not appear to offer much variety, but there's some clever tech behind their futuristic design. Each one comes with an iPad, which you can use to set mood lighting, mood music, and even your morning alarm. King-sized beds are made up with Italian linens, and soundproofing means you feel like you're staying in a boutique hotel rather than a modern behemoth. The large lobby-lounge, where you check yourself in via a touchscreen, has communal iMacs as well as superfast wi-fi. It's split into cozy sections for reading and relaxing, and thanks to shelves stacked with secondhand books and a mix of brightly cultured Vitra chairs and sofas, it feels homely yet functional. There's also a superb bar—smarter than you'd expect given the room prices.

Hotel Amour

Best for bohemians on a budget

8 rue de Navarin, 9th

hotelamourparis.fr

Don't rock up at Hotel Amour with grand ideas of romance. Despite its name, you won't find the four-poster beds and luxe bathrooms you might be imagining. This one-of-a-kind hotel is part-owned by graffiti artist André Saraiva, and it's filled with mid-century antiques, retro flea market finds, and cheeky artwork. Rooms kick off at less than €100 a night, and include both great-value singles with queen-sized beds and more luxurious superior and duplex options. It's known for its bistro and adjoining jungle-like courtyard where you can settle in for everything from Sunday brunch to a glass of wine. House cocktails give a nod to the hotel's amorous theme—think Unchained Passion and Last Tango in Paris.

C.O.Q Hotel Paris

Best for no-frills luxury

15 rue Edouard Manet, 13th

coqhotelparis.com

This hotel offers exceptional value in the south of Paris, with rooms usually *just* dipping beneath the €150 mark. The slightly odd name stands for Community of Quality, a nod to both their communal spaces and high-end service and furnishings. There are welcome drinks on arrival, bathrooms stocked with Rituals products, and well-decorated rooms painted in smart deep grays and blues. It might look like Scandinavian influences are at play, but furniture and linens have been sourced from France wherever possible. C.O.Q also manages to straddle the line between catering to informal business travelers and vacationers, with movie screenings and occasional game nights as part of the mix.

Hôtel Paradis

Best for short-term stays

41 rue des Petites Écuries, 10th

hotelparadisparis.com

Boutique hotels around the Grands Boulevards tend to be *très cher,* but rates at this Dorothée Meilichzon–designed three-star hotel, located closer toward Gare du Nord and Gare de L'Est, can be great value. It's a step down the price and service ladder from a true boutique hotel, but it still has plenty of style. Rooms are small but smart with slightly retro touches like padded headboards, and service is reliably switched on. If you want to settle in for a week of luxury, it's not the right spot, but it's an excellent short-break choice if sightseeing, shopping, and dining out are at the top of your agenda. A short walk west takes you to the city's top department stores, while to the east you're on the doorstep of the slightly gritty but up-and-coming Faubourg Saint-Denis.

BOUTIQUE

Le Pigalle

Best for rock 'n' roll romance

9 rue Frochot, 9th

lepigalle.paris

Stay right in the heart of the SoPi bar action—and in sight of the Sacré-Cœur's gleaming domes—at this hip yet affordable design hotel that's low-key enough to be relaxing while still feeling special. One of its biggest selling points is its restaurant and bar, where they hold events and pop-ups while serving a core menu of substantial bar snacks and cocktails: think salads, arancini, and tartines. Each room is designed individually and has loads of personality, with art and photography hung gallery-style on the walls. The simplest have an in-room iPad for choosing your tunes; some of the more expensive have turntables and a selection of vinyl records. Other highlights include claw-foot tubs and whisky-stocked in-room bars. To get the amenities you want, check which room you're reserving before you book. Inexplicably, one room is done out with bunk beds, for a "fun dormitory-type experience."

Hôtel Le 123 Sebastopol

Best for movie fans

123 boulevard de Sébastopol, 2nd

astotel.com

Hôtel Le 123 Sebastopol is the pick of the Astotel group's selection of reliable, modern hotels—but don't think that means you'll be staying in an identikit chain. This is their best-located property in Paris, and it's dedicated to all things cinema. That means spotlights illuminating the bar, fold-down movie theater seats to perch on at breakfast, and oceans of golden-age movie memorabilia. Some rooms are small, but they go above and beyond on things that really make a difference: free non-alcoholic drinks in the mini bar; light, bright design; and the option to drop into any of their other hotels for complimentary drinks. Deluxe rooms with balconies are the pick of the bunch, and if you really want to splash the cash you can book out their private cinema. There's no on-site restaurant, but you're just a short walk from some of the city's best dining.

Hôtel JoBo

Best for je ne sais quoi–style

10 rue d'Ormesson, 4th

hoteldejobo.paris

Hôtel JoBo, named after the charismatic Empress Joséphine Bonaparte, Napoleon Bonaparte's first wife, has playfully transformed a 17th-century convent into a bijou Marais bolthole. It's completely over-the-top, but somehow still just about tasteful. Striped wallpaper clashes with leopard-print chairs, and flamboyant floral curtains hang next to gold-embossed wooden headboards. It won't be to everyone's taste, but this hotel doesn't make compromises when it comes to design. Service, by contrast, is attentive and considerate with plenty of extras that go the extra mile: iPads to rent, fresh flowers on request, and a knowledgeable concierge service. The rooms are luxurious, with fine linens and fancy coffee machines. Despite its diminutive size, the hotel also has a bar and tearoom—both just as outrageously furnished—and a small patio open in summer.

The Hoxton

Best for the in-crowd

30–32 rue du Sentier, 2nd

thehoxton.com

With its beautiful, light-filled bar-atrium and impeccably designed rooms, the Hoxton is spearheading the renaissance of the neighborhood around Sentier. As the name suggests, the first Hoxton hotel was in East London, but the Brit-owned group quickly expanded across Europe with their winning formula: stylish rooms cleverly priced by size (ranging from "shoe-box" to "biggy"), and plush bars and restaurants that draw in locals and visitors alike who are keen to see-and-be-seen. Exposed wood floors combined with touches of velvet and leather make the design contemporary but warm, and bathrooms are fresh and light in white tile. Extras like late checkout for €10 an hour are indicative of their approach to flexible travel, but for some the service might be too cool for school.

Edgar

Best for understated design

31 rue d'Alexandrie, 2nd

edgarparis.com

Unlike other international imports nearby, this little design hotel is as French as they come, each of the 12 rooms individually designed by the family and friends of owner Guillaume Rouget-Luchaire. There's a photographer's darkroom created by designers Pascal Brault and Stéphane Lubrina, and a safari-style room inspired by photographer Yann Arthus-Bertrand's time in the Maasai Mara. The hotel sits at the heart of a micro-quartier that was once the city's garment district, but like many neighborhoods around Sentier it's quickly being overtaken by start-up culture and cool restaurants. Despite its diminutive size, the hotel even has two of the latter: Baretto, a casual Italian bistro, and the eponymous Edgar, where the menu is heavy on sustainable seafood and comfort-cooking classics. If the idea of shunning crowded hotel lobbies and tour groups appeals, then you can't find a better spot.

Le Citizen Hôtel

Best for canalside cool

96 quai de Jemmapes, 10th

lecitizenhotel.com

You'll need to book early to snag a room at this canal-side townhouse hotel, *the* spot to stay near the Canal Saint-Martin. Not only do you have superb bars and restaurants on your doorstep, but all rooms have views over the water—offering fascinating people watching at any time of the day. The decor is simple, but with so much to see out the window, the emphasis is on relaxation rather than boundary-pushing style. Breakfast is included in the room prices, whether you go down to the buffet or have breakfast in bed, and includes everything from homemade yogurts and compotes to crêpes and granola. In the evening, they offer happy-hour drinks and tapas. Just don't confuse Le Citizen with international chain citizenM; this hotel is independently run.

Hôtel Caron de Beaumarchais

Best for Parisian atmosphere

12 rue Vieille du Temple, 4th

carondebeaumarchais.com

How much chintz is too much chintz? It's a difficult balance to strike, but this hotel gets it just right. There is a hint here and there—draped floral curtains and traditionally upholstered chaises longues—yet mostly Hôtel Caron de Beaumarchais just feels delightfully French. Somehow seamlessly blending 18th-century design influences with modern amenities such as bedside USB charging points, it's tenuously themed around *The Marriage of Figaro*, a play written by Pierre-Augustin Caron de Beaumarchais mere steps away in 1785. In practice, you'll find it's simply an intimate and memorable 19-room hotel with the feel of an upscale B&B. The best rooms overlook the street, with small sun-drenched balconies where you can have breakfast in the morning. Unusual for Paris, le petit déjeuner is served here until noon. Best of all is the location, which is plumb in the center of the Marais.

Le General Hotel

Best for slick modern design

5–7 rue Rampon, 11th

legeneralhotel.com

Between the Marais and the Canal Saint-Martin, this contemporary and midsized four-star hotel is minimalist without being clinical, and smart without being business-y. The odd retro touch adds a bit of character, but generally rooms are white, light, and bright—ideal if relaxation is your top vacation priority after days spent exploring Paris. In-room massages can be booked to guarantee a good night's sleep, while Nespresso machines will help break your slumber in the morning. There's no on-site restaurant, but you'll get a smartphone loaded with local recommendations. Rooms can be a steal outside of high season, sometimes less than €150 a night, although that figure can double in busy periods.

1K

Best for South American–inspired chic

3 boulevard du Temple, 3rd

1k-paris.com

Sure, a hotel with its own Mezcaleria might not have been what you pictured for your Parisian trip—but 1K is here to tempt you away from traditionalism, albeit at a price. Influences are drawn from Peru to Mexico, and a party vibe pervades throughout, from the street-facing bar to the two rooftop suites with private plunge pools. The other 50 rooms are simple and airy, and there's a small gym if you need to burn off last night's pisco sours; you've also got some of the Haut Marais's best bars on the doorstep. Book ahead for the best rates, sometimes below €200 if you get lucky.

Grand Pigalle Hôtel

Best for golden-age glamour reinvented
29 rue Victor Massé, 9th
grandpigalle.com

Just down the street—but not associated with—Le Pigalle is this swish designer hotel. Above its classy lobby cocktail bar are just 37 rooms all done out in rich gray and navy tones with gold accents and graphic wallpaper. The Manhattan-meets-Paris vibe isn't unintentional; it's run by the Experimental Group, the folks who are also behind New York's Compagnie des Vins Surnaturels as well as the Experimental Cocktail Clubs in London and Paris. The concept here is "bed and beverage," but think late nightcaps sipped on velvet sofas and soundproofed rooms designed for a restorative night's sleep rather than a post-party crash. This was the group's first hotel, but their empire is steadily growing. Try their nearby Hotel des Grands Boulevards if you'd like to be a little closer to the center of Paris.

Hôtel Jules & Jim

Best for Haut Marais hipsters
11 rue des Gravilliers, 3rd
hoteljulesetjim.com

This arty hideaway is in the heart of the Haut Marais, steps from the best specialty coffee shops and boutiques. Black and white photography hangs above the beds, and the hotel showcases the work of a new artist in its ground-floor gallery each year. Film buffs will also spot that the hotel is named after François Truffaut's celebrated film of the same name. Rooms vary from cozy, modern doubles to cocoon-like "Hi-Macs"; there are also two small rooftop rooms with balconies. Although there are just 23 rooms, extras are plentiful: There's 24-hour room service, a sleek bar, and city tours on offer for around €200 via the hotel's own vintage Citroën DS.

Hôtel Adèle & Jules

Best for style with soul

2 Cité Rougemont, 9th

hoteladelejules.com

Parisian hotels are often hip but rarely homely. Family-run Adèle & Jules, opened in 2016, set out to bring a little more warmth to the boutique hotel scene. Its 60 rooms are split across two 19th-century buildings, and designer Stéphane Poux hasn't been afraid to use a bit of color in her modernization: Teal headboards contrasted against bold wallpaper prints give rooms the feel of a luxury apartment. Crisp white bedding and subway-tile bathrooms complete the picture. The overall emphasis here is on relaxation and peace: It's the kind of spot you come to laze in a fluffy robe and order breakfast in bed.

BLOW-THE-BUDGET

Hôtel du Petit Moulin

Best for a romantic hideaway

29 rue de Poitou, 3rd

hotelpetitmoulinparis.com

If you're going to throw your budget out the window, you might as well do it somewhere that's completely one of a kind. The Hôtel du Petit Moulin, disguised as a backstreet Marais bakery, is about as special as high-end boutique hotels come. From the street there's little to let on that this is actually a hotel; the boulangerie's original façade and signage still remain. Inside, it's a different story. The Christian Lacroix–designed interiors blend baroque and rococo influences with modern luxury; it's bright and colorful with a sense of fun. There are just 17 rooms, offering rare seclusion, although the other trappings of five-star hotels (fancy restaurants, concierge services, and the like) are understandably absent. They make up for it with a menu of bespoke add-on experiences ranging from in-room massages to macaron-making classes and city tours in a vintage Citroën 2CV.

OFF Seine

Best for scene-seekers
86 quai d'Austerlitz, 13th

offparisseine.com

Staying in a floating hotel on the Seine, complete with a miniature infinity pool dropping away to the river, is an experience you simply can't re-create anywhere else. This hotel is as cool as they come, bobbing just off the bank near the Gare d'Austerlitz on a stretch of riverside now throbbing with bars and clubs at the weekend. The 54 rooms are sleek and comfy in relaxing monochrome tones, though not particularly spacious. The best rooms have Seine vistas. In the evening you can book private cruises up the river to the Eiffel Tower, while the bar keeps things busy with a regular roster of DJs and events; plenty of people just visit for a cocktail (or three). In summer there's even a pop-up seafood terrace, La Mer à Boire.

Hôtel Bel Ami

Best for upscale elegance
7 rue Saint-Benoît, 6th

hotelbelami-paris.com

If you want to stay in the heart of Saint-Germain, you can expect to pay for the privilege—and that means some hotels rest on their laurels knowing that they can get away with high prices and old-school service. This isn't the case at the Starwood-owned Bel Ami, which manages to balance nods to area's bohemian past with seamless five-star luxury. Traditional trappings include 24-hour room service, understated design, a fitness center, and a Carita-stocked spa. Less expected is that the hotel is pet friendly, even offering babysitting services for dogs and little ones alike. Just in case you're feeling a little too at home, the bar and restaurant are reassuringly expensive, but with so many super spots just a few minutes' walk away, you're unlikely to frequent them more than once.

Maison Souquet

Best for all-out hedonism

10 rue de Bruxelles, 9th

maisonsouquet.com

Once dubbed the sexiest hotel in Paris, Maison Souquet will live up to your every expectation of Belle Époque glamour in Paris. This former brothel has been completely reinvented by Jacques Garcia to re-create the atmosphere of early 20th-century Montmartre, with opulent fabrics, low-lit wood-paneled lounges, and oodles of velvet—everywhere from the curtains to the furniture. Despite mixing Moorish, Japanese, and French influences, it comes together as one magical and cohesive whole. This is a temple to hedonism, so get ready to tumble down the rabbit hole. If you tear yourself away from your room, the private spa (key on request only) has an indoor pool and hammam, and there's an intimate bar where even the cocktails are named after famous courtesans.

Le Bristol

Best for all-out luxury

12 rue du Faubourg Saint-Honoré, 8th

oetkercollection.com

There's a lot of choice when it comes to fabulous five-stars in Paris, but Le Bristol is the grande dame to rule them all. Understated elegance and refined opulence have been the hotel's signatures since it opened on glitzy rue du Faubourg Saint-Honoré in 1925—along with a fastidious approach to service. Beyond the marble lobby, overseen by the hotel's fluffy Burmese cat Fa-Raon, is a smart courtyard garden where tea is served beneath crisp white parasols. It's overlooked by plush, antique-filled rooms and suites that are traditional but not old-fashioned—the largest coming in at a whopping 2,700 square feet. For dining, there's a choice of the three-Michelin-star restaurant, Epicure; the one-Michelin-star restaurant, 114 Faubourg; and 24-hour room service. But perhaps the best perk is the covered rooftop pool, where you can take a dip after a La Prairie spa treatment as you look out over the Eiffel Tower and Sacré-Cœur.

ACKNOWLEDGMENTS

A very grand merci to my editor, Róisín, and The Countryman Press team. It's long been my dream to write this guide, and it's been a pleasure to work with you. Thank you so much for being so enthusiastic about this title, and for the great design, editing, and cartography.

To Helena Staniszewska, who put me at ease behind the camera wandering the backstreets of Montmartre, a big thanks for taking my author picture on a chilly winter day in January.

Many thank yous are due in Pairs. First, to Iz, for everything. Not least booking a ticket to visit before I'd even booked my own to move here. I can't imagine the past ten years without you. Second, to the awesome wine(ing) crew, for adventures that make me fall in love with Paris again and again each week. And to all the friends who've come to stay, championed this book, or helped me research along the way—each cocktail, wine, and menu tip is tied to great memories. Meme, my French fashion and theatre education is all thanks to you; thank you for being a creative inspiration.

I'd also like to say a huge thanks to the many editors, colleagues, and friends who've commissioned me to write about Paris and encouraged me over the years. Particularly to George, who preordered this guide before I even knew it was on sale and without whom I wouldn't have moved here for the first time on sabbatical.

Lastly, above all, to Rosemary and Alan, for their support and love (and some early proofreading).

INDEX